Functions of English
Student's Book

Second edition

Functions of English

A course for upper-intermediate and more advanced students

Student's Book

Leo Jones

with cartoons by Peter Kneebone

SECOND EDITION

Cambridge University Press
Cambridge
New York   New Rochelle
Melbourne   Sydney

Published by the Press Syndicate of the University of Cambridge
The Pitt Building, Trumpington Street, Cambridge CB2 1RP
32 East 57th Street, New York, NY 10022, USA
10 Stamford Road, Oakleigh, Melbourne 3166, Australia

© Cambridge University Press 1977, 1981

First published 1977
Fifth printing 1980
Second edition 1981
Sixth printing 1987

Printed in Great Britain
at the Bath Press, Avon

ISBN 0 521 28249 7 Student's Book
ISBN 0 521 28248 9 Teacher's Book
ISBN 0 521 23836 6 Cassette

Recorded Exercises
ISBN 0 521 28382 5 Student's Workbook
ISBN 0 521 26353 0 Set of 3 cassettes

Copyright
The law allows a reader to make a single copy of part of a book for purposes of private study. It does not allow the copying of entire books or the making of multiple copies of extracts. Written permission for any such copying must always be obtained from the publisher in advance.

FP

Contents

Introduction to the student 1

1 Talking about yourself, starting a conversation, making a date 3

2 Asking for information: question techniques, answering techniques, getting more information 9

3 Getting people to do things: requesting, attracting attention, agreeing and refusing 14

4 Talking about past events: remembering, describing experiences, imagining 'What if . . .' 20

5 Conversation techniques: hesitating, preventing interruptions and interrupting politely, bringing in other people 25

6 Talking about the future: stating intentions, discussing probability, considering 'What if . . .' 30

7 Offering to do something, asking permission, giving reasons 36

8 Giving opinions, agreeing and disagreeing, discussing 41

9 Describing things, instructing people how to do things, checking understanding 46

10 Talking about similarities, talking about differences, stating preferences 51

11 Making suggestions and giving advice, expressing enthusiasm, persuading 58

12 Complaining, apologizing and forgiving, expressing disappointment 64

13 Describing places, describing people 70

14 Telling a story: narrative techniques, handling dialogue, controlling a narrative 76

15 Dealing with moods and feelings: anger, sadness, indifference. Saying goodbye 82

Communication activities 89

Acknowledgements

Thanks again to the following friends and colleagues who gave me so much advice and encouragement in the development of the first edition of this book: John Forster, Sue Gosling, Diana Maddock, Michael Roberts, Rob Shave, Ken Tooke, Karen and Peter Viney, Katy Walker, Sally and Guy Wellman.

Many thanks to all my colleagues, old and new, who helped me to test this second edition so thoroughly, spotted the things which were not quite right and suggested numerous improvements. And thanks to all the students from all over the world who used it and made their comments. And a big thank you to Kay McKechnie for guiding the book so efficiently and understandingly through its final stages. Finally, many, many thanks to C. von Baeyer, whose painstaking and imaginative work on the forthcoming North American edition has contributed so many improvements to this British edition.

The author and publishers are grateful to the following for permission to reproduce illustrations:
David Redfern Photography (page 11); Ethan Russell (page 11); National Film Archive (page 24); Camera Press Ltd (page 24); Barnaby's Picture Library (page 72); Swiss National Tourist Office (page 72); Pan American World Airways (page 74); Posy Simmonds (page 80); United Feature Syndicate Inc. (page 85); Scotcade Ltd (pages 90, 98, 111 and 128); Thomson Travel Ltd (pages 119 and 133).

Drawings by: Leslie Marshall (page 56); Ted Draper (pages 105 and 123); Dave Parkins (pages 116 and 133)
Cover photographs by John Walmsley
Book design by Peter Ducker

Introduction to the student

Please read this introduction carefully to get to know the aims and methods of this book.

Who is this book for?

Functions of English is for upper-intermediate and more advanced students who feel confident about using basic English grammar and vocabulary, and who are now ready to learn more about using English in real-life situations.

What does this book cover?

For your English to be effective, it must be appropriate to the situation you are in. So, when you are trying to choose the best way to express yourself in a particular situation, you have to keep in mind several things:
— What are you trying to do with your English? Are you describing something, persuading someone, giving your opinion, or what? These are called *language functions*.
— What sort of person are you in this situation? Is your *role* friend, stranger, employee, customer?
— Where are you talking? Is the *setting* on a plane, at a party, at a meeting?
— What are you talking about? Is the *topic* business, travel, sport?

The units in this book cover the main language functions, and the exercises involve all sorts of people in all sorts of places and talking about all sorts of topics. You will be practising both the English that you know already, and some useful new ways of saying things.

This book is just the starting point though. There are many places in the book where you may want to ask your teacher for more information, or for more time to practise something new.

How is this book organized?

Each unit in *Functions of English* is divided into several sections:

Conversation

This illustrates how each function could be carried out during a conversation. Don't read the transcript in the book until you've listened to the tape at least twice. This is *not* a 'dialogue' which you have to learn by heart.

Presentation

The presentation sections include descriptions of the functions and various ways of carrying them out. You should read each presentation section *before* your teacher goes through it with the class. Then you should keep your book closed while the teacher presents the ideas using the board and the tape and asks you for your ideas. There are usually three presentation sections in a unit. Make sure your pronunciation of the new expressions is good enough.

Practice

There are several practice sections after each presentation. The first one is often controlled by the teacher, so that you have a chance to ask for help and advice. In the other practice sections the class is divided up into pairs or small groups of students who work on their own. Try hard to use new expressions that you have just met in the presentation section.

Communication activities

Many exercises tell you to look at a particular number in the *Communication activities* section at the back of this book. These activities involve two or more people communicating with each other in discussions, role-plays, problem-solving activities, etc. Each person or group has different instructions, printed on different pages so that the participants can't see each other's instructions. In this way you can have information that is different from your partner's information, just as in most real communication outside the classroom.

Please, don't prepare the communication activities ahead of time – let them be a surprise. And don't look at your partner's instructions – keep the activities spontaneous.

Try to experiment with different ways to get your point across in these activities. Be as talkative as you can – never just say 'Yes' or 'No'. And don't be afraid to make mistakes – learn from them! Your teacher will be going around from group to group to listen and help. At the end of each activity, the class will discuss difficulties, and the teacher will point out serious mistakes that would make a listener misunderstand something.

Written work

The written work at the end of each unit gives you further practice of some important items from the unit. Again in the written work, try to experiment with new ways of communicating.

This book may be a little different from what you are used to. Don't be surprised – a course that teaches conversation must be a little unpredictable, since real-life conversations are so often unpredictable. We hope that you find working with this book interesting and enjoyable.

1 Talking about yourself, starting a conversation, making a date

1.1 Conversation

Richard: Excuse me, anyone sitting here?
Jane: Um, no, no. Oh! Er ... I'll just move my bag.
Richard: Right, thanks.
Jane: There we are!
Richard: Thank you ... Oh, nice day, isn't it?
Jane: Oh, it's lovely, yes. It does make a change, doesn't it?
Richard: Let's hope it'll last.
Jane: Mm, mm.
Richard: What ... what's that book you're reading? Looks ... looks really interesting.
Jane: Oh, it's ... called *Life on Earth*. Um, I got it because ... er ... because of that ... um ... television programme.
Richard: Oh yeah.
Jane: Did ... did you see it? A few ... a few weeks ago?
Richard: No, no, I didn't see it – I remember it, but I didn't see it, I'm afraid.
Jane: Yes, about how life began. It's ... it's fantastic. I'm ... I'm reading it as well because I've got a project at school – I'm a teacher.
Richard: I see, I see.
Jane: And it's really useful for background research – it's lovely.
Richard: Yes, I like ... I like a bit of telly really. I like the old movies best of all ...
Jane: Oh, yes. So do I.
Richard: The old films.
Jane: Yes, yes. They're on very late, though. I don't see a lot of them, because ... [*fade*]
Jane: ... but I don't go to the cinema a lot, there just isn't time.
Richard: Well, I'm going tonight, in fact.
Jane: Tonight? Oh, are you?

Richard: Yes, most nights really.
Jane: What are you going to see?
Richard: The new Clint Eastwood film.
Jane: Oh, lovely!
Richard: You wouldn't like to come, would you? Why don't you come as well?
Jane: Oh, that would be nice, yes! Oh, why not? ... Oh, oh dear, I'm busy tonight, I'm afraid. What about tomorrow night? Is that any good to you?
Richard: Oh dear, no, I'm afraid I'm busy then myself.
Jane: Oh ... well ...
Richard: Well ... we ... obviously it'd be nice to meet sometime. Er ...
Jane: Yes.
Richard: Er ... perhaps if you gave me your phone number I could ... we could fix something up?
Jane: Oh, yes, alright. Well, shall I write it down for you?
Richard: Sure, yes.
Jane: OK ...
Richard: Good heavens! I should have been at the office ten minutes ago!
Jane: Oh dear.
Richard: Er, look, I'll ... I'll ... that's the number, is it?
Jane: Yes, here you are.
Richard: Thanks, I'll ... I'll give you a ring then and ... and we'll sort something out.
Jane: Alright.
Richard: Right, well, it's been very nice meeting you.
Jane: Yes!
Richard: Byebye, then!
Jane: Yes, byebye!
Richard: Byebye!

 1.2 Presentation: talking about yourself

The presentation sections in this book usually give you some *new* expressions to learn. But for now we'd like you to concentrate on using the English you know already. The aim of the next three practice sections is to give you a chance to get used to the methods that will be used throughout this book. Try to ask as many short questions as possible to get as much information as possible from your partner. Try to answer in long sentences, keeping talking; do not just say '*Yes*' or '*No*'. If you are in doubt about what to say or how to continue, ask your teacher.

1.3 Practice

Get together with another student. Introduce yourselves first and then find out as much as you can about each other.
Here are some ideas to start you off, but ask for as much detail as possible when you get interested. Don't accept short, safe answers. Ask about his or her:

FAMILY Brothers and sisters. Parents. Childhood – happy? Home – where does he or she live?

4

FRIENDS	Many or just a few? What do they talk about and do together? Is it easy to make new friends?
EDUCATION	Different schools, colleges or universities. Favourite subjects at school and why. Diplomas, degrees and paper qualifications. Future plans.
EMPLOYMENT	Present job. What exactly does he or she have to do? Advantages and drawbacks. Previous jobs – details. Future plans.
FREE TIME	Hobbies. Sports. TV, radio, cinema. What does he or she do at weekends and in the evenings? What does he or she like reading?
TRAVEL	Countries visited. Parts of own country he or she knows. Languages. Favourite sort of holiday. Future plans.

When everyone has finished tell the whole class the most interesting things you have found out about your partner.

1.4 Practice

Get together with a different student from the one you talked to in 1.3. Look at the questionnaire on page 6. Help each other to fill in the details requested. Discuss how to answer the more difficult questions.
When you have finished, compare your answers with another pair of students. Give your completed questionnaire to your teacher to read and correct.

1.5 Practice

Imagine that you are at a cocktail party with the rest of the class. At a cocktail party everyone stands with a drink, chats for a few minutes to one guest and then is expected to *circulate* and move on to another guest. The host or hostess (your teacher) normally speeds up the circulation by introducing guests to each other.
Now stand up and have a party! Talk to as many people as possible.

QUESTIONNAIRE

Surname...

First names in full...

Nationality..

Permanent address..

....

Present address...

....

Occupation or field of study...

....

Secondary education...

....

Qualifications...

Further education and language courses..

What foreign languages do you speak and how well?...

....

Have you ever lived in an English-speaking country? If so, how long for?......................................

....

What English course books have you used?...

....

When do you (or will you) need to use English?..

....

What aspects of your English need improving most?..

....

What are the main things you hope to get from this course?..

....

1.6 Presentation: starting a conversation

It is often difficult to make contact with strangers who speak another language. Unless, that is, you have a few opening gambits up your sleeve!
Here are some useful ways of starting a conversation with a stranger:

What a nice day, isn't it?
Dreadful weather, don't you think?
Excuse me, is anybody sitting here?
Excuse me, haven't we met somewhere before?
Sorry, I couldn't help overhearing – did you mention something about . . . ?
Excuse me, have you got a light by any chance?
Excuse me, could you tell me the time?
Er, could you help me, I'm trying to find my way to . . .

Decide when these opening gambits would be appropriate. And how you might continue after. Think of some situations where you might use each opening gambit.

1.7 Communication activity

To practise ways of starting conversations, the class is divided into two groups: group A and group B. If you are in group A, look at communication activity 151; if you are in group B, look at communication activity 38. The communication activities are at the back of the book.

1.8 Presentation: making a date

After you have made contact and had a short conversation, you may want to arrange another meeting. These are expressions you can use to arrange to meet someone:

Oh, um, are you doing anything this evening, by any chance?
Um, I was thinking of going to the cinema this evening, would you like to come?
Er, are you going to be busy this evening? I was wondering if you might like to come to the cinema with me.
I'm going out to the theatre with some friends. Would you like to join us?

YES! *That'd be lovely.*
I'd love to.
How nice of you, thanks very much.
Mmm, that's a great idea.

NO! *Oh, dear, I'm afraid I'm busy tonight.*
Tonight's difficult. Perhaps tomorrow evening, though.
I'm sorry, I'm expecting some visitors this evening.
This evening's a bit of a problem. What about tomorrow?

Decide when each of these expressions would be appropriate and what you might say before and after. Think of some possible situations in which you would use each expression.

1.9 Practice

Build conversations like this from the prompts below, using expressions presented in 1.8.

A: I'm going out for a walk on Sunday. Would you like to join me?
B: Oh, dear, I'm afraid I'm busy on Sunday.
A: Perhaps some other time then.
B: Sure. Thanks for asking me, though.

cinema	picnic
theatre	walk
drink	swimming
meal	drive
dancing	London

1.10 Practice

Get up again and try to make a date with the people you contacted earlier. One way to begin might be: *'Oh, it is nice to see you again. How are you?'*

Keep experimenting and practising until you feel comfortable with the expressions in this unit.

1.11 Written work

Discuss each of these with your teacher before you do them yourself. Decide how best to approach each one:

1. Imagine two people meeting for the first time and write the conversation between them in dialogue form.

2. Imagine you are writing your first letter to an English pen-friend. Introduce yourself, so that he or she has an impression of what sort of person you are.

3. Write a letter inviting an English acquaintance to spend the weekend with your family.

2 Asking for information: question techniques, answering techniques, getting more information

2.1 Conversation

Stranger: Excuse me.
Resident: Yes?
Stranger: I ... I was wondering if you could help me.
Resident: Well, I'll try.
Stranger: I need to find out where the ... er ... town centre is. Now I see there's a sign up there that points to the left.
Resident: Ah well, let me see ... er ... it all depends if you're on foot or going by car.
Stranger: Ah no, I'm walking.
Resident: Ah well, you turn to the right and then carry straight on.
Stranger: Ah, right, thanks! Er ... I wonder if you could tell me ... um ... if there's a good hotel ... er ... in town that I can use.
Resident: Oh, let me think a moment ... um ... yes, there are two hotels – they're in the High Street ... er ... one on each side of the road.
Stranger: Right, well, I expect we'll manage to find one of those. Er, I wonder if you could tell me ... er ... anything about the ... er ... castle in town ... er ... where ... where it is.
Resident: Um, well, it's actually further on ... er ... down the High Street and then you cross over the bridge and it's on the other side of the river.
Stranger: I see, I see. Could you tell me a bit more about it? Is it interesting? Is it old?
Resident: I'm not really sure. I've never actually been there myself. It ... yes, I think it's quite old, I think it's about ... um ... 500 years old – something like that.
Stranger: Worth ... worth visiting, you think?
Resident: Well, it's one of the tourist attractions of the town ... um ...

Stranger: I see, I see.
Resident: I've no idea, I'm afraid. As I say, I've never been there.
Stranger: I see. Do you happen to know when it's open?
Resident: Er ... I'm not really sure ... um ... I think it depends on ... er ... what time of year you go ... um ... as to whether it's open.
Stranger: Well, right, thank you, thank you.
Resident: Er, excuse me, I hope you don't mind my asking, but ... um ... your voice interests me ... er ... do you mind if I ask ... er ... where you come from?
Stranger: No, no, no. I come from Wiltshire.
Resident: Ah!

2.2 Presentation: question techniques

A conversation often depends on questions to keep it going in the direction you want it to go. The one who asks the questions in a conversation usually controls the conversation. Various techniques may be necessary to get different sorts of information from different people. Most people are very polite in the way they ask a stranger about something – if you are more direct, you may appear to be very rude! Anyway, personal questions have to be expressed tactfully. Here are some useful opening expressions you can use to lead up to questions:

I was wondering if you could help me. I'd like to know ...
I wonder if you could tell me ...
This may sound a stupid question, but I'd like to know ...
Excuse me, do you happen to know ...
Would you mind telling me ...
I hope you don't mind my asking, but I'd like to know ...
Something else I'd like to know is ...

Decide when such expressions might be appropriate. They are also useful as 'hesitation devices' to give you time to prepare your thoughts!

2.3 Practice

Note down about five pieces of factual information and five pieces of personal information you would like from your teacher. Take turns asking your teacher questions: remember to be very polite when asking for personal information. When you have finished, ask a partner similar questions.

2.4 Presentation: answering techniques

You may often need to delay answering a question while you think for a moment or check on your facts. Here are some useful techniques for delaying your answer:

Well, let me see ...
Well now ...
Oh, let me think for a moment ...
I'm not sure, I'll just have to find out ...
That's a very interesting question ...

Or you may want to avoid answering altogether, using expressions like these:

I'm not really sure.
I can't tell you off-hand, I'm afraid.
I'm terribly sorry, I really don't know.
I've no idea, I'm afraid.
I can't answer that one, but I'll tell you where you can find out.
I'd rather not answer that, if you don't mind.

Decide when you might use these expressions. Think of some situations when they would be appropriate.

2.5 Practice

Now your teacher is going to ask you questions like the ones you asked in 2.3. Try to delay or avoid answering them.

2.6 Communication activity

Work in pairs. Each of you has different information about the career of the Beatles. One of you should look at activity 40, while the other looks at activity 109.

2.7 Presentation: getting more information

When you ask people questions, they often don't give you enough information right away. You may have to ask them for additional information – you may want further details or you may not be satisfied with the answer given.
Here are some techniques for getting the extra information you want:

Could you tell me a bit more about . . . ?
Sorry, but I'd like to know some more about . . .
I didn't quite follow what you said about . . .
Sorry, that's not quite what I meant, what I really wanted to know was . . .
Sorry to press you, but could you tell me . . . ?
Sorry, I don't quite understand why . . .

Decide when these expressions would be used and what might be said before and after.

2.8 Practice

Get your teacher to give you as much information as possible about his or her:

Education   Favourite way of spending weekends
Professional career so far   Favourite way of spending evenings
Favourite holiday resort

Try to get as many details as you can!

2.9 Communication activity

Work in groups of four (or three). What do you know about the famous people on English banknotes?

Each of you is an expert on one of them. Student A should look
at activity 99, student B at activity 92, student C at activity 44 and student D at
activity 8.

2.10 Practice

Work in pairs or small groups. Ask each of your partners to give you as much information as possible about his or her:

Town
Country
A place in Britain he or she knows
Job or field of study
Family and friends
Hobbies
Sports activities

Deal with each topic by asking your partner(s) questions.

2.11 Written work

This section concentrates on asking for information in letters.
Discuss the special techniques involved with your teacher before doing the written work.

1 Write a letter to the Hotel Romantica to find out about their prices and facilities. You are thinking of taking your family to spend a fortnight there.

2 Write a personal letter to a former colleague asking how he or she is getting on and saying how life has changed since you last saw each other three years ago.

When you have written the letters, deliver them to another student. He or she should then write replies to the letters.

3 Getting people to do things: requesting, attracting attention, agreeing and refusing

3.1 Conversation

Brenda: Ah, right, here we are!
Bob: This is the place I was telling you about.
Brenda: Yeah, could you ask the waiter if we can sit near the window?
Bob: Er, yes, of course. Er, waiter!
Waiter: Good evening, sir.
Bob: We'd like to sit near the window if that's possible.
Waiter: Er... Ah!... er... I'm afraid all the tables there are... are taken. Would you mind sitting near... nearer the bar?
Bob: Oh, yes, alright. That suit you?
Brenda: Mm, fine.
Bob: Good.
Waiter: Thank you, sir.
Bob: Now let's have a... er... oh, I... I don't seem to have any cigarettes on me. Have you got a cigarette, by any chance?
Brenda: I'm awfully sorry, but you see I've given up.
Bob: Oh, you've stopped smoking at last. Well done!... Oh well, let's have a look at the menu, then. Um... oh, there isn't a menu... er... er, do you think you could ask the people at the next table if we could look at their menu?
Brenda: Yes, of course. Um... excuse me, could you possibly let us see your menu? Oh, they haven't got one either.
Bob: Er, oh, I'll... I'll ask these people at this table. Um, I wonder if you could possibly let us have a look at your menu... Thank you!... Ah, here we are, then. Now, what's on? Um... oh, 'Soup of the Day' – well, I wonder what that is.

Brenda: I wonder what 'Mexican Dressing' is.
Bob: Oh, sounds interesting ... er, where's the waiter gone, we'll order ... er ... I can't see ...
Brenda: He's over there.
Bob: Oh, could you possibly catch his eye?
Brenda: Yeah. Um, waiter!
Waiter: Yes, madam.
Bob: Ah, waiter ... um, I wonder if you could tell me what 'Soup of the Day' is, please.
Waiter: Certainly, yes. 'Soup of the Day' is Cream of Asparagus.
Bob: Ah, that sounds nice!
Brenda: Mm, could you tell me what 'Mexican Dressing' is?
Waiter: Ah, 'Mexican Dressing', yes. That's one of our specialities. That's hot, spicy and sweet. It's very nice, I recommend it.
Brenda: Oh!
Waiter: Er ... now ... could I ... I wonder if I could possibly ask you to move to a table near the window after all? It's ... er ... it turns out the manager tells me this table's reserved.
Brenda: Oh, yes, sure.
Bob: Of course, by all means.

3.2 Presentation: requesting

When you want someone to do something for you, there are many English expressions you can use. Some of these expressions are too polite for some situations. Other expressions sound rude in particular situations.

The right expression to use depends on
   a) How difficult, unpleasant or urgent the task is.

   b) Who you are and who you are talking to – the roles you are playing and your relationship.

15

Here are some useful ways of requesting. They are marked with stars, according to how polite they are.

★   *Hey, I need some change for the phone.*
Oh, dear, I haven't got any change for the phone.
I don't seem to have any change on me.

★★   *You haven't got 10p, have you?*
Have you got 10p, by any chance?

★★★   *You couldn't lend me 50p, could you?*
Do you think you could lend me 50p?
I wonder if you could lend me 50p?

★★★★   *Would you mind lending me £1?*
If you could lend me £1, I'd be very grateful.

★★★★★   *Could you possibly lend me your typewriter?*
Do you think you could possibly lend me your typewriter?
I wonder if you could possibly lend me your typewriter?

★★★★★★   *I hope you don't mind my asking, but I wonder if it might be at all possible for you to lend me your car?*

Decide when you would use these expressions. Can you add any more expressions to the list?

3.3   Practice

Because your tone of voice is extremely important when you ask someone to do something, this section should be done with your teacher. You may need to be corrected frequently at first.

Treat your teacher as an acquaintance, not a close friend. Ask him or her to lend you these things:

5p	umbrella	stamp
20p	watch	comb
£2	bicycle	diary
£20	rubber	dictionary
£200	pen	nailfile

Now ask him or her to do these things:

open the window halfway – open it all the way – close it
open the door – half close it – close it
move his chair – move it elsewhere – move it back again
explain these words – 'role', 'deferential', 'urgent'
fetch you a drink, a sandwich, a newspaper, some cigarettes
give you a cigarette, a light, a piece of paper, a testimonial

3.4 Communication activity

Begin working in pairs. You will be asking people to do different things for you. One of you should look at activity 80 and the other at activity 47.

3.5 Practice

So far you have practised different request expressions depending on how difficult, unpleasant or urgent the task was. We are now going to look at the second variable: the roles you are playing and your relationship. Your teacher is going to play a number of different roles (see below), each one for a few minutes. Get him or her to do some of the same things you wanted done in 3.3. By the way, there may be some tasks it is not appropriate to even ask to be done!

receptionist in a hotel
your boss in an office
your secretary in an office

your best friend
your father (or mother)-in-law-to-be
an elderly stranger
a child

3.6 Communication activity

Begin working in pairs. You will be asking different sorts of people to do things for you. Decide which of you is A and which is B. A should look at activity 41, and B at activity 61 (you will have to meet up with other student Bs to decide which role to play).

3.7 Presentation: attracting attention, agreeing and refusing

If you want to talk to someone it may be necessary first to attract their attention in a polite way. Also *you* are likely to be asked to do things which you may agree to do – or want to *refuse*.

To attract someone's attention:

Er, excuse me . . .
Er, I say . . .
Er, Mr Jones . . . (if you know someone's name)

To agree:

Sure.
I'd be glad to.
Why, yes of course.
By all means.

To refuse:

I'm awfully sorry, but you see . . .
I'd like to say yes, but . . .
I'd really like to help you, but . . .

British people don't like to refuse bluntly (in a plain, direct way). Instead, they usually give an excuse so as not to hurt people's feelings. These excuses are sometimes called 'little white lies'; but of course they shouldn't involve serious or obvious lying.

3.8 Practice

Build conversations like this from the prompts below, using the expressions presented in 3.7:

A: Er, excuse me . . .
B: Yes?
A: I wonder if you could lend me your dictionary – I'm doing my homework.
B: I'd like to say yes, but I'm using it myself. Perhaps later.
A: Oh, I see, never mind. Thanks anyway.

open the door	correct the spelling in a letter for me
lend me the newspaper	type an application form for me
give me a cigarette	give me a lift home
get me a cup of coffee	arrive on time
pass the salt	write more clearly
tell me the time	speak more slowly

Try to use a variety of expressions!

3.9 Communication activity

Begin working in pairs. You will be asking strangers to do things for you. One of you should look at activity 53, and the other at activity 1.

3.10 Communication activity

Work in groups of two or three. This activity consists of three separate situations. One of you (A) should look at activity 93 and the other(s) (B and C) at activity 17.

3.11 Written work

Discuss these ideas with your teacher before you start writing:

1 You have a rich uncle. You want him to lend you some money so that you can buy a new car. He knows you crashed your old one. Write him a letter asking him to lend you the money. Give reasons.

2 You have an irresponsible nephew (or niece). You have just received a letter asking for money to buy a new car. Reply as you think fit.

3 Write in dialogue form the first part of one of the conversations you had in 3.10.

4 Talking about past events: remembering, describing experiences, imagining 'What if...'

4.1 Conversation

Bob: Didn't you once go sailing? On a holiday or something?
Jane: Oh, yes!
Bob: Tell me about it.
Jane: I'll never forget the time I first went, actually. Um... I set off from the shore to get to the boat in a little dinghy...
Bob: Yes.
Jane: ... with an engine. And that was fine, I was chugging along and about halfway there I suddenly noticed that water was coming in at the bottom.
Bob: Oh, what did you do?
Jane: Er... I looked around to see if there was a bucket – I could chuck it over the side – and all there was in fact was a sort of shovel thing. So...
Bob: Oh, what hap... what happened next?
Jane: Well, I started shovelling water out and... um... oh yes, the... the next thing that happened was that the engine stopped, so there...
Bob: Uh! How did you feel about that?
Jane: Oh, terrible! And I'd never been sailing before...
Bob: Yes.
Jane: I couldn't even swim, actually. And I didn't know what to do... um... as far as I remember, I... I started shouting and whistling and nobody took any notice.
Bob: Yes.
Jane: Um... and... oh, then I... then I... then I used the shovel as a... as a... as a paddle – started paddling on either side – and I slowly got towards the boat...
Bob: Yes, yes.

Jane: And occasionally chucked some more water over the side as I went.
Bob: Er... why didn't you call out to the boat and get them to come and help you?
Jane: Well, I tried but they... I think they were having a party and just couldn't hear me or something.
Bob: Oh, I see!
Jane: And... er...
Bob: What would you have done if there hadn't been anything to paddle with?
Jane: I don't know! I'd... I suppose I'd have used my hands or I'd have just sat there shouting at the top of my voice until eventually someone would have rescued me.

4.2 Presentation: remembering

Different sorts of questions can help people to remember things that happened. If you want specific information you need to use questions like these:

What happened next?
Had you already...?
Were you going to...?
What were you doing while...?
Then what did you do?
Why didn't you...?
How did you feel when...?
Did you think of...?

Decide when these questions would be most useful. Think of examples.

Here are some expressions that are often used to answer specific questions:

As far as I can remember...
I remember quite clearly that...
After that...
Before that...
While that was happening...
The next thing I did was to...

Decide how these answers could continue.

4.3 Practice

Do you remember your first day at school? Can you remember any details?
What do you remember about your first English lessons?
Do you remember your first visit abroad?
Do you remember the first time you went away from your family?

Try to get everyone in the class (including your teacher) to answer each of these questions – then help them to remember more details by asking questions like the ones suggested in 4.2.

4.4 Communication activity

Work in pairs. Each of you will be finding out what your partner ('an aquaintance') did yesterday. One of you should look at activity 23, and the other at activity 79.

4.5 Practice

Work in small groups. Help each other to remember as much as possible about these topics:

Your last holiday
The last time you were interviewed
The most exciting sporting event you've seen
Your earliest memory

Report the most amusing or interesting details back to the rest of the class.

4.6 Presentation: describing experiences

It is often interesting to find out about other people's experiences. Here are some questions which can help people to remember experiences which they had almost forgotten:

Have you ever...?
Tell me about the time you...?
I hear you once...?
Didn't you once...?
You've..., haven't you?

And we sometimes begin talking about our experiences like this:

Oh, that takes me back.
I'm not sure I can remember all the details, but...
I'll never forget the time I...
That reminds me of the time I...

Decide how you could continue from these openings.

4.7 Practice

Work in groups of three or four. In each group, ask each other questions to help you to remember some amusing or unpleasant experiences:

An unusual job you once did
A crime you witnessed or were the victim of
The longest or worst journey you've been on
An accident you saw or which happened to you
Your driving test or first driving lesson

Shopping or eating out in a foreign country
A coincidence which happened to you or someone you know

Report the most interesting story back to the rest of the class.

4.8 Presentation: imagining 'What if...'

Often when we are recalling past events or experiences, we speculate 'what might have happened otherwise'. Coincidences happen, we make decisions, things just happen – but what would have happened if the situation had been different?

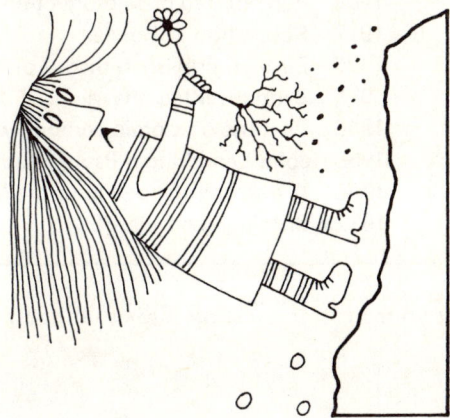

Here are some ways of encouraging people to imagine:

What would you have done if...?
What might have happened if...?
How would you have felt if...?

Here are a few possible ways of beginning answers:

Oh, I don't know, I suppose I might have...
Difficult to say, but I think I'd have...
Well, of course, I could have...

Make sure you can easily pronounce the expressions, and that you are sure when to use them.

4.9 Practice

Think of four or five very different places in the world. What would have been *different* about your life so far if you had been born and brought up there? Talk about these aspects with the rest of the class:

Childhood   Medical care
Education   Employment prospects
Family life   Entertainment

Try to use the expressions introduced in 4.8 appropriately.

4.10 Practice

Here are a number of events which affected the course of world history. In groups of three or four, speculate what might have happened if these events had not taken place. Try to imagine *several* consequences of each event and what would have happened if all these things had not happened.

2,000,000,000 BC	First life on earth.	1865	Lincoln abolished slavery in USA.
20,000 BC	First writing.	1875	Bell invented the telephone.
8,000 BC	Wheel invented.	1879	Edison invented the electric light.
5,000 BC	Britain became an island.	1903	Wright Brothers' first powered flight.
800 AD	Paper money first used.	1908	Ford started mass production of Model T car.
1327	Guns first used in battle.	1917	Revolution in Russia.
1455	First book printed by Gutenberg in Germany.	1920	Einstein published theory of relativity.
		1926	Baird invented television.
1492	Columbus discovered America.	1945	First use of atomic bomb in war.
1556	Tobacco introduced to Europe.	1956	John Lennon met Paul McCartney.
1815	Napoleon defeated at Waterloo.	1969	Armstrong stepped onto the Moon.
1818	Karl Marx born.	1972	Britain joined the EEC.

When you have finished, report your most interesting ideas to the rest of the class.

4.11 Practice

In small groups, talk about the holiday you remember best. Find out as much as you can about each other's holiday – including the things that might have gone wrong.

4.12 Written work

Discuss these ideas before you begin writing:

1 Write a letter to a friend about a trip you went on recently, or about the day you described in 4.4, or about what you did last weekend.
2 You saw one of these people at a party, but you were too shy to talk. Write down what might have happened and what you would have said if you had felt more confident.

3 Begin a short narrative with this opening line:
   I'll never forget the day ...

5 Conversation techniques: hesitating, preventing interruptions and interrupting politely, bringing in other people

5.1 Conversation

Anne: Listen, everyone! I'd like to make a suggestion... Now, how about having a party soon? Not... not this weekend – it's too soon, but say... next Saturday. Well?
Brenda: Why not?
Charlie: Yes, sure.
Anne: Well, what do you think, Brenda?
Brenda: Well... yeah, but why do you want to have one?
Anne: Oh, I don't know really... er... how shall I put it? Well, we've been together for quite a long time, haven't we? The four of us... in the flat. Well, it's nearly five years, I think, isn't it?
Charlie: Yeah, about that.
Brenda: It must be.
Anne: I think that's worth celebrating... Don't you agree, Charlie?
Charlie: Yes, I do actually. I think it'd be a good idea. But... er... there are one or two points I'd like to make, actually. Um... quite strongly. First is: invitation only. Everyone should have an invite, otherwise we'll get a lot of gatecrashers. OK? Yeah, yeah. And the other thing is: everyone brings a bottle, otherwise it'll cost a fortune...
Brenda: And another thing: I think we should have food, otherwise it's just going to be a drinking party...
Charlie: Yeah, yeah, sorry to interrupt. If we are going to have food, the thing is I want to know who's going to prepare it. I mean it's all very well saying 'have food' but it's again a lot of work and a lot of money...

Brenda: If I could just come in here ... I've just got a new recipe book and I'd kind of like a chance to try out a few things, you know. So ...
Charlie: Great!
Brenda: ... I'll do the food.
Charlie: Well, that sounds great. Marvellous. That's lovely.
Anne: Derek, you're being very quiet. What have you got to say?
Derek: Well ... er ... you know ... um ... although it should be a lot of fun ... er ... I think it's going to be a lot of hard work, as well. Um ... and that ... the thing is, you see, what worries me is ... er ... um ...
Charlie: What?
Derek: ... the clearing-up afterwards.
All: Ahh! Aha!
Derek: I really detest clearing up. So if we were to get that sorted out ...
Anne: Well, let's see now. I think I've got quite a good idea to solve that one.
Charlie: Mm?
Anne: If we wait till the very end, there's going to be a few people left over and we can ask *them* to do the clearing-up before they go home.
Charlie: Great!

5.2 Presentation: hesitating

Hesitation is a natural part of using a language – both for those learning English as well as for native speakers. Very articulate and fluent speakers don't need to hesitate very often. But most people need to hesitate quite a lot during a conversation.
The worst way to hesitate is with silence. Silence causes embarrassment and confusion. Silence also lets other people speak rather than you.
Hesitation devices give you time to think – to organize your thoughts and decide how to express them. Here are some useful hesitation devices:

um
er
well
actually
in fact
you see
you know
the thing is
how shall I put it
let's see now
it's like this, you see
sort of
the lengthened to *theee*
a lengthened to *ayyy*
to lengthened to *tooo*

Decide when these hesitation devices might be useful. You may have strong feelings about 'bad English' – get them off your chest before you begin the practice!

5.3 Practice

Give a one-minute, totally unprepared talk to the rest of the class on one of these subjects. Choose the subject you know *least* about! The idea is to keep talking constantly and *not* be silent while you are thinking. In fact you should try to give as little information as possible! The best way to start is '*Well, I've been asked to talk about . . .*'

Babies	Communism
Breakfast	Tourism
Trees	Vegetarianism
Coffee	Nudism
Drugs	Classical music
Electricity	Literature
Hitch-hiking	British politics
The Sun	The Queen of England
The Moon	Insects

Make sure you and the others in the class are using a *variety* of hesitation devices – not just '*um*' all the time!

5.4 Presentation: preventing interruptions and interrupting politely

Even if you pride yourself on being a 'good listener', there will be times when you want to keep talking and not be interrupted. Here are some useful techniques to make sure you continue to hold the floor and are not interrupted:

There are two points I'd like to make . . .
   (You can't be easily interrupted till you have made them both!)
Although . . .
   (You can't be easily interrupted until you have spoken two clauses.)
And another thing . . .
   (You can't be easily interrupted until you have added a sentence.)
Pausing in the middle of a sentence, not between sentences.
   (You can't be easily interrupted until you have completed your sentence.)

If you want to interrupt politely when another person is speaking, you need to be alert for suitable opportunities. This may take a lot of practice. If you break in at the wrong time, you may be considered aggressive. The end of a sentence is often a polite place to break in – but not always (see above!). Here are some useful techniques for interrupting:

If I could just come in here . . . (formal)
Sorry to interrupt, but . . .
I'd just like to say that . . .
Um . . . um . . . um . . . (repeated until the speaker lets you speak)
By the way . . . (to change the subject)
That reminds me . . .

Discuss these techniques as a class, think of some examples, and make sure your intonation and tone of voice are alright.

27

5.5 Communication activity

Work in groups of three or four. You will be presenting a point of view about 'Smokers' rights' and later about 'Work' – if you can prevent your partners' interruptions! To begin, student A should look at activity 50, student B at activity 20, student C at activity 74 and student D at activity 107. When you have finished, discuss what you did with your teacher and the rest of the class. You may decide you need to change roles and 're-play' the discussions, presenting different points of view.

5.6 Presentation: bringing in other people

Actually, you probably don't want to appear to dominate people all the time! You may want to hear other people's views and make sure everyone gets a chance to speak in a conversation. A chairman at a meeting can just nominate speakers or point to them, but in a conversation we use less direct methods:

Don't you agree, John?
What do you think, John?
You're very quiet, John.
I expect John will agree with me when I say . . .
John's looking sceptical.
I don't know what John thinks, but . . .
I think John knows more about this than I do.

Decide what the effect of each of these techniques would be.

5.7 Practice

Work as a 'committee' of four or five. Make sure that each member of the committee has a chance to state his or her views on *each* aspect of this topic:

THE PROBLEMS OF OLD PEOPLE

When you are ready, report your discussion to the rest of the class. Then deal with this topic in the same way:

TRAFFIC IN CITIES

5.8 Communication activity

Work in three groups. Each group will be working as a 'committee'. Students in group A should look at activity 35, group B at activity 75 and group C at activity 101.

5.9 Written work

The techniques used in this unit are conversation techniques and they are not generally used in writing except when you are:
    writing a dialogue, or
    writing a friendly personal letter.
In both cases, conversational phrases only serve the function of making things seem more natural or intimate.

Discuss each of these ideas with your teacher before you start writing:

1. Imagine you are on the phone to a friend talking about what you both did today and yesterday. Write *only your side* of the conversation in dialogue form.

2. Write the other side to another student's telephone conversation. See if you both have the same ideas!

3. Write a chatty personal letter to a good friend explaining why you didn't meet him or her as arranged yesterday. Invent some good excuses!

6 Talking about the future: stating intentions, discussing probability, considering 'What if...'

6.1 Conversation

Richard: Hallo Bob!
Bob: Hallo, Richard!
Richard: How are you?
Bob: Alright. Are you?
Richard: Yes, fine thanks.
Bob: Good.
Richard: Bit fed up with this weather.
Bob: Oh, yes, yes.
Richard: You...er...taking a holiday this year?
Bob: Er...yes, I'm hoping to take three weeks in May and then have another three weeks later on in the year – September, possibly.
Richard: Good, good, good. Do you think you'll be going away or staying at home?
Bob: Oh, I don't think I'll go away in May. Doubt if I'll have enough money saved up by then.
Richard: What about in September?
Bob: Oh yes, I'm definitely going abroad then – if I can afford it. I haven't quite made up my mind where though. Greece, maybe. Or Spain – Italy. Bound to be hot and sunny out there.
Richard: Yes. Suppose you...er...couldn't afford it?
Bob: Oh...er...I expect I'd stay at home and just have days out at the coast or in the country, you know.
Richard: Just supposing you had all the money in the world, where would you go?
Bob: Oh...I...yes, I think I'd go to Canada. Yes, I've always wanted to go there.

Richard: Marvellous!
Bob: Well... how about you? Do you think you'll go abroad this year?
Richard: Yes. Booked up already. We're going to... um... going to Norway in August... going walking.
Bob: Really? Oh, what's the weather like out there at that time of year?
Richard: Oh, you never know with Norway. I wouldn't be surprised if it rained!

6.2 Presentation: stating intentions

Nothing is totally certain about the future. We can try to foresee events, we can make plans and state our intentions – but we can never be sure what will actually happen. Here are some ways of stating intentions and showing how firmly we intend to do something. They are all phrased as answers to the question: *'Are you going to...?'*

✓	YES, DEFINITELY:	*Nothing's going to stop me... -ing...*
		I'm certainly going to...
		I'm going to..., that's for sure.
✓?	YES, PROBABLY:	*I think I'll...*
		I may well...
		I'm hoping to...
??	PERHAPS:	*I'm thinking of... -ing...*
		I thought I might...
		I haven't made up my mind whether to...
✗?	NO, PROBABLY NOT:	*I don't think I'll...*
		I don't really feel like... -ing...
		I'm not really planning to...
✗	NO, DEFINITELY NOT:	*I'm certainly not going to...*
		You won't catch me... -ing...
		I'm not going to... if I can help it.

Decide how you might use these expressions when talking about your plans for this evening. Be careful about your pronunciation and tone of voice!

6.3 Practice

Look at this list of countries. Check the list through and decide how firmly you intend to visit or don't intend to visit them in the next few years. Use the categories suggested in 6.2.

Canada	Spain	Switzerland	Australia
Mexico	Scotland	Venezuela	Japan
Brazil	Ireland	Portugal	Sweden
China	Italy	Nigeria	USA

Tell the rest of the class about your intentions.

6.4 Practice

Work in small groups. Talk about your intentions of visiting the countries which are nearest to your own country. Ask each other questions like:

Why?
Why not?
Why aren't you sure?
If you go there, what towns are you going to visit?

6.5 Communication activity

Work in three groups. Each group will be planning a different journey. Group A should look at activity 31, group B at activity 3 and group C at activity 143.

6.6 Practice

Think about your plans for this evening, this weekend and your next holiday. Get together with two or three other students and discuss your plans. Talk about what you plan *not* to do, as well as what you intend to do.

6.7 Presentation: discussing probability

Often we have no control at all over what will happen. But we can try to judge whether something is likely to happen or not. We can even claim to be totally certain. Here are some ways of stating probability. They are all phrased as answers to the questions: *'Do you think it will . . .?'*

✓	YES, DEFINITELY	*Of course it'll . . .* *It's sure to . . .* *It's bound to . . .*
✓?	YES, PROBABLY	*I expect it'll . . .* *I wouldn't be surprised if it . . . -ed* *I bet it'll . . .*
??	PERHAPS	*There's a chance it'll . . .* *It might possibly . . .* *I suppose it might . . .*
✗?	NO, PROBABLY NOT	*I doubt if it'll . . .* *I don't think it'll . . .* *There's not much chance of it . . . -ing*
✗	NO, DEFINITELY NOT	*Of course it won't . . .* *There's no chance of it . . . -ing.* *I'm absolutely sure it won't . . .*

Decide how you would use the expressions to talk about *tomorrow's weather*. How important is the tone of voice that is used? How much do you believe someone who claims to be absolutely sure?

6.8 Practice

Look at Madame Zoë's predictions for the future. Work in small groups and discuss how probable you think each of her predictions are. When you are ready report your assessment of her predictions to the rest of the class.

Madame Zoë's predictions

```
1982  England will win the World Cup.
1983  An Englishman will become world heavyweight boxing champion.
1984  War in South Africa: Whites v. Blacks.
1985  A woman will become US President.
1986  Police force in UK will be armed.
1987  A colony will be established on Mars.
1988  War in Asia: China v. Russia.
1989  Britain will become a republic.
1990  Marijuana will be legalized in Britain.
1992  Cure for cancer will be discovered.
1995  War in Europe: Russia v. The Rest.
1997  War in South America: USA v. The Rest.
1999  World peace and prosperity will be restored.
2000  World government will be established.
2011  World oil supply will dry up.
2013  English will become the only language in the world.
2020  Package tours to the Moon will begin.
```

6.9 Practice

Prices of most things have gone up a lot in recent years. Can you predict how much these items will cost in five years time?

box of matches	stamp for letter abroad	family car	video recorder
20 cigarettes	local telephone call	1 litre petrol	quartz wristwatch
pair of shoes	cup of coffee	colour TV set	paperback novel

Begin in three groups, decide on your prices. Then rearrange yourselves into three new groups to discuss your figures with students from the other groups.

6.10 Practice

What changes do you expect to occur in Britain, in your country and in the world during the next fifteen years? How different will everyday life be then?
Begin your discussion in groups, then report your predictions to the class.

6.11 Presentation: considering 'What if...'

Everything we have done so far in this unit is about the uncertain future. We can never be sure about what will happen in the future. But sometimes we day-dream about things that are *extremely unlikely* to happen and then imagine the consequences. Here are some ways of encouraging someone to day-dream:

Just imagine if you became a millionaire ...
Suppose you came into a lot of money ...
Just supposing you won the football pools ...

And we ask someone to talk about the day-dream with questions like these:

... what would you do?
... how would you feel?
... what would it be like?

The answers to these questions often begin like this:

Oh, I suppose I'd ...
Oh, I might ...
Oh, I think I'd ...
Oh, I expect I'd ...

Notice that if we are talking about *possible* future events we normally say, for example:

A: *If you pass the exam, how will you feel?*
B: *Oh, I suppose I'll be pretty pleased.*

Decide what kind of events are either extremely unlikely or in fact possible, and when the expressions would be used. Think of some examples.

6.12 Practice

Build conversations like this from the prompts below, using the expressions in 6.11:

A: Suppose you got a pay rise tomorrow, how would you feel?
B: Oh, I expect I'd feel very happy indeed.
A: I think I would, too.

got married
had your car stolen
found a £5 note
lost your wallet
failed an important exam
met the Queen of England
witnessed a murder
became a beauty queen
became homeless
inherited £1 million

Try to use all the recommended expressions.

6.13 Practice

Work in small groups. What would you do if one day you were in each of these situations? How would you feel? What would it be like?

Let your imagination take over and talk about the details of your life which would be different. Report your best ideas to the rest of the class.

6.14 Practice

Work in small groups. Decide on your own personal plans for the next few days *and* your ambitions for the future. Talk about events that you think will happen *and* things that probably won't happen.
Compare your own plans and ambitions with your partners' plans and ambitions. When you have finished, look at communication activity 9.

6.15 Written work

1 Write a letter to a friend describing your plans for your next holiday.

2 Write a description of the world at some time in the future. Choose your own date.

3 If you became president of your country one day, what changes would you make?

7 Offering to do something, asking permission, giving reasons

7.1 Conversation

Richard: Well, that was delicious! Thanks very much indeed ... I didn't know, you're a really good cook, aren't you?
Brenda: Thank you.
Richard: If you like, I could do the washing-up.
Brenda: No, don't bother, I can do it myself later.
Richard: Alright ... er ... do you mind if I smoke?
Brenda: Yes, go ahead!
Richard: Oh, I've lost ... left my cigarettes in the hall.
Brenda: Shall I get them for you?
Richard: Er ... no, no ... oh look, it's alright – I've got another packet here.
Brenda: Let me get you an ashtray.
Richard: Thanks.
Brenda: Would you like me to make coffee now?
Richard: Yes! Thanks! Um ... look, I wonder if I could possibly use your phone?
Brenda: Oh, I'm sorry, that's not possible. You see, it's out of order again.
Richard: Oh, n ... er ... well, it's rather complicated, but you see I promised to phone a colleague before nine and I see it's now about five to ... um ... er ... would you mind very much if I went down the road to the phone box?
Brenda: Oh, it's about ten minutes' walk away. If you like, I could drive you there.
Richard: Oh, would you? Thanks!
Brenda: Yes, certainly.
Richard: Thanks!
Brenda: I'll make coffee later, when we get back.
Richard: Right!

7.2 Presentation: offering to do something

When something needs to be done you can ask someone else to do it, or offer to do it yourself or just do it without saying anything. If someone else is doing something, you can offer to help.
Here are some useful ways of offering to do something:

Let me get it for you.
Shall I get it for you?
Any point in my getting it for you?
How about my getting it for you?
Would you like me to get it for you?
If you like, I could get it for you.
Can I help you with that?

We might accept such offers with answers like:

That's very kind of you, thanks.
Oh would you? Thanks.
Thanks a lot.

Or refuse them by saying:

No, don't bother, I can do it myself.
No, it's alright, I can manage.
Thanks ever so much, but it's alright, really.

Decide when you would use each of the expressions.

7.3 Practice

Talk to your teacher and make some helpful offers to cope with his or her problems. Your teacher is bored, ill, lonely, thirsty, depressed, unfit, hard-up, hungry, and over-worked. If you have time, do this with another student, too.

7.4 Communication activity

Work in pairs. You will be offering to help each other with various difficulties. One of you should look at activity 91, and the other at activity 63.

7.5 Presentation: asking permission

Sometimes you need to do more than just offer to do something – you may need to ask permission to make sure you are allowed to do it. The expression to use depends on:
a) The type of task you want to do and the trouble you may have getting permission to do it.
b) Who you are and who you are talking to – the role you are playing and your relationship.

Here are some useful ways of asking permission. The expressions get more and more polite as you go down the list:

I'm going to ...
I thought I might ...
I'd like to ...
Alright if I ...?
Anyone mind if I ...?
D'you mind if I ...?
Is it alright if I ...?
Would it be alright if I ...?
Would you mind if I ...?
I wonder if I could possibly ...?
I hope you don't mind, but would it be at all possible for me to ...?

We tend to give permission in just a short phrase, like:

OK.
Yes, go ahead.
Yes, I suppose so.
Oh well, alright.

And we refuse permission like this:

That's not a very good idea.
No, please don't.
I'd rather you didn't if you don't mind.
I'm sorry, but that's not possible.

Decide when you might use each of the expressions. Give examples of each expression in use.

7.6 Practice

Make a list of five things you would like to do, but which you have to get your teacher's permission for. Ask for permission to do them – watch out, your teacher may ask you *'Why?'*! Later your teacher will change roles and play the role of the head of the school, so you may then need to change the way you ask.

7.7 Presentation: giving reasons

When you ask someone for permission, he or she is likely to ask you *'Why?'*. Here are some useful ways of explaining your reasons:

Well, you see . . .
The reason is . . .
Well, the thing is . . .
My reason for asking is this . . .
It's because . . .
It's rather complicated but you see . . .
. . . and that's why I'd like to . . .
. . . and that's my reason for asking if I can . . .

Decide how you would give reasons using these phrases. Imagine you want to borrow various things from your teacher. What would you say?

7.8 Practice

Build conversations like this from the prompts below:

A: Would it be alright if I left the room for a moment, you see I have to make a phone call?
B: I'd rather you didn't if you don't mind, you see this is a very important part of the lesson.
A: Oh, alright, I see.

leave room
smoke my pipe
borrow car
take day off
open window
have coffee break
borrow umbrella
use phone
watch TV
borrow book

Imagine that you are talking to an acquaintance, rather than a close friend.

7.9 Communication activity

Work in pairs. You will be playing several different roles during this activity. One of you should look at activity 11, and the other at activity 56.

7.10 Communication activity

Work in groups of three. One of you (student A) is about to move into a new flat and a lot of things need doing. You each have a whole day free to do the work together.

Student A should look at activity 105, student B at activity 73 and student C at activity 19.

7.11 Written work

Discuss these ideas with your teacher before you start writing:

1 A friend of yours is leaving the country unexpectedly. Write a letter offering to help with last-minute packing, travel arrangements etc.

2 Write a letter on behalf of your class to the parks department of your town requesting permission to hold a barbecue in a local park. Then 'deliver' it to another student, who will write the parks department's reply.

3 Write a letter to a friend who owns a weekend cottage in the country asking him if you can spend a few days with some friends there. Then 'deliver' it to another student, who will write your friend's reply.

8 Giving opinions, agreeing and disagreeing, discussing

8.1 Conversation

Bob: Now, I'd just like to say that I think that ... er ... this government proposing to build more nuclear power stations in this country is ... really being stupid ... um ... The point about nuclear power is that we haven't learnt to do ... er ... away with the waste. We haven't learnt to cope with the waste of it yet.
Liz: Well, I sometimes think that, you know, they've got an impossible job. I mean ... I mean ... all the impression I get is that there is no alternative – that's the impression I get.
Bob: No, no, no I ... I ... I don't agree with that at ... at all. There's plenty of alternatives. There's the sun – solar power ... um ...
Richard: Um ... um ... excuse ...
Bob: ... that is a source that is always there, we always have it.
Richard: I don't ... I don't quite see what you're getting at, actually – 'solar power', what's that?
Bob: Well ... um ... the heat from the sun, it can be used in solar panels on the tops of houses for heating ... um ... storing up ... er ... er ... power to heat water and to heat the houses ... er ... you know, some places have ... er ... solar panels in operation already and they are saving money ... um ...
Liz: That's a good point actually, but is it ... is it really viable, that, I mean because I'd ...
Bob: Surely, it must be!
Richard: That's just what I was thinking, you see.
Bob: It must be. Er ... and the one ... er ... great advantage is, that I can see, if

>
> the government set up small units to build solar panels and to install them, then it would be creating employment – which would ease the unemployment situation ... terrific advantages.
>
> Richard: I ... I ... I don't quite follow what ... what ... where it's all ... where we're all headed anyway. I mean what ... what ...
>
> Liz: No and I've heard ... I mean ... I've heard that in England, I mean, there's not enough sun, is there? For, I mean, solar panels here? Doesn't that ...
>
> Bob: Yes, well, that's not quite true. I ... erm ... there's ... there's quite a bit of sun – you may not feel the actual heat of it on some occasions ...
>
> Liz: No, you're right there!
>
> Bob: ... but the light power ... er ... from the sun will ... er ...

8.2 Presentation: giving opinions

When you are taking part in a discussion it is useful to have techniques up your sleeve for getting people to listen to you and to give yourself *thinking time* while you arrange your ideas. Here are some useful opening expressions graded according to how formal they are:

INFORMAL
If you ask me ...
You know what I think, I think that ...
I'd say that ...
The point is ...
Wouldn't you say that ...
Don't you agree that ...
As I see it ...
I'd just like to say that I think that ...
FORMAL *I'd like to point out that ...*

Decide when the different expressions would be appropriate. Do you agree with the order they have been put in? Can you suggest more expressions?

8.3 Practice

Build conversations like this from the prompts below, using the expressions presented in 8.2:

A: How do you feel about dogs?
B: Well, if you ask me, dogs are a nuisance.
A: Why do you think that?
B: Because they have to be taken for walks and eat a lot of food and ...

dogs	travel abroad
cats	learning Latin
parking	home video recorders
women drivers	transistor radios
capital punishment	children

Try to use new expressions each time!

8.4 Practice

Work in groups of three. Find out each other's opinions on these subjects:

Holidays	Inflation
Birthdays	Air travel
Christmas	Television
Politeness	Winter sports
Esperanto	Communism

Report your partners' opinions to the students in another group.

8.5 Presentation: agreeing and disagreeing

Here are some useful ways of agreeing or disagreeing with someone's opinion. Notice that you need to be very *polite* when disagreeing with someone in English – even someone you know quite well.

AGREEMENT
I couldn't agree more.
That's just what I was thinking.
You know, that's exactly what I think.
I agree entirely.
That's a good point.

DISAGREEMENT
Yes, that's quite true, but ...
I'm not sure I quite agree ...
Well, you have a point there, but ...
Perhaps, but don't you think that ...
I see what you mean, but ...

If you know someone *very well* you can disagree more directly using expressions like these:

I can't agree with you there.
You can't be serious!
Come off it!
Don't be so silly!

8.6 Practice

Here is a series of extreme opinions:

'Learning English is pointless'
'Britain is unpleasant to live in'
'Football is boring'
'Marriage is out of date'
'Space travel is a waste of money'
'Strikes should be made illegal'
'All motorists should be obliged to wear seat belts'
'There should be a 50 km speed limit on all roads'
'English is a very easy language to learn'

Build conversations about each topic, using the expressions presented in 8.5. Follow this pattern:

A: It says here that learning English is pointless!
B: I'm not sure I quite agree, I'd say it was very worthwhile.
A: Why do you think that?
B: Well, because English is a world language – you need it to communicate with people from other countries.
A: That's just what I was thinking.

8.7 Communication activity

Work in groups of three. Each of you will be giving and reacting to opinions. Student A should look at activity 70, student B at activity 30 and student C at activity 7.

8.8 Presentation: discussing

In a friendly discussion you don't want to present your opinions so strongly that you start an argument. For example, you may want to express an opinion in a more tentative way, like this:

I sometimes think that ...
Well, I've heard that ...
Would you agree that ...?
Do you think it's right to say that ...?

And you may want to ask other people to explain their point of view more exactly using expressions like these:

I didn't quite follow what you were saying about ...
I don't quite see what you mean, I'm afraid.
I don't quite see what you're getting at.

And other people may not understand what you say to *them*. So you may need to rephrase your own statements, beginning like this:

That's not quite what I meant ...
Let me put it another way ...
Sorry, let me explain ...

Decide how you would use these phrases in a discussion about a topic in the news today.

8.9 Communication activity

Work in pairs. Each of you will have a different topic to prepare and present your views on. One of you should look at activity 142, and the other at activity 102.

8.10 Practice

Work as a large group. Pick one of these topics and discuss it, making sure each member of the group gets a chance to speak!

Pollution
Fashions
Tourism

Make notes on the points that are made.

8.11 Practice: debate

Begin by choosing a motion everyone is interested in. Then spend some time preparing your ideas (perhaps in small groups). Then choose a chairman and opening speakers for and against the motion. First the opening speakers present their opposing opinions on the motion. Then the discussion is 'open to the floor' and everyone else can give their opinions.

8.12 Written work

Talk about these ideas with your teacher before you write anything:

1 Your teacher has been asked to write a confidential report giving his or her opinion on your character and work. Write the report you would *like* to have.

2 From the notes you made in 8.10, write a report of the discussion.

3 Write your opinions about a topic that is in the news, or a topic you have discussed in this unit.

9 Describing things, instructing people how to do things, checking understanding

9.1 Conversation

Jane: Hallo, Bob!
Bob: Hallo!
Jane: I've just bought a new cassette recorder at last.
Bob: Oh, you've got it!
Jane: Yes.
Bob: Oh!
Jane: So you can borrow it any time you like.
Bob: Right, thanks very much ... how big is it? What size is it?
Jane: Oh, quite small. It'll fit into ... into my bag.
Bob: Ah, yes, and what's it made of?
Jane: Plastic and ... er ... some chrome.
Bob: Yes ... erm ... what does it look like?
Jane: Well, do you want to see it? I've got it with me now.
Bob: Uh ... have you? Yes please, yes.
Jane: Here you are!
Bob: Thanks.
Jane: There it is!
Bob: Oh, that's a very smart machine!
Jane: It's good, isn't it?
Bob: Yes! And ... er ... how does it work?
Jane: Yes, I'd better tell you, hadn't I? In case you're going to borrow it. Um ... well, the first thing you have to do is ... er ... to make sure it's plugged in or got batteries. OK?
Bob: Oh, I see, you can use it either ...
Jane: Yes.

Bob: I see.
Jane: Um... and then the next thing you do is take your tape, press this button here...
Bob: Yes.
Jane: And slot it in there. OK?
Bob: I see.
Jane: Oh, by the way, don't forget to put it in the right way round, just in case the tape gets jammed up...
Bob: Sorry, I'm not quite clear on...
Jane: Well, just put it in this way up and...
Bob: Oh, I see. Oh, I see. So the cassette faces that... Yes, I see.
Jane: Yes, that's right. And then close the lid and just press the play button...
Bob: I see.
Jane: Are you with me?
Bob: What do you have to do to record?
Jane: Er... well, it's exactly the same thing, only you press that button there instead.
Bob: I see.
Jane: Do you see what I mean?
Bob: Yes, you don't have to press the record and the play button together to record?
Jane: No, no, no, no, not on this model, no... um...
Bob: Uhhu... I'm not quite clear... um... where's the microphone? If you just want to record the voice?
Jane: Oh, that's just down here. There, do you see?
Bob: I see, yes.
Jane: Um... and the volume control is here.
Bob: Yes, yes.
Jane: OK?
Bob: And where... could you tell me where you put the batteries in if you...
Jane: Oh, yes... er... they go in at the back just there.
Bob: Ah, I see!
Jane: Oh, and one thing I must ask you. Be careful not to leave it switched on because... um... it can get overheated. OK?
Bob: Right! Right, thanks.

9.2 Presentation: describing things

You may often have to describe an object, or a piece of equipment or a machine or gadget to people. You may need to do this because your listener is unfamiliar with the object, or because you cannot think of the name for it.

In describing an object we often have to answer questions like these:

What size is it?
What shape is it?
What colour is it?
What's it made of?
What does it look like?
What's it used for?
How does it work?

Decide how you would answer these questions in describing the objects around you in the classroom. Are there any other important questions missing from the list?

9.3 Practice

Here are some objects and gadgets to describe. Try to give a detailed description, bearing in mind the questions suggested in 9.2:

the Union Jack	a tape recorder
your national flag	a wristwatch
a tin opener	a zip fastener
an egg-timer	a pair of skis
a deckchair	a razor

Get other students and your teacher to help if you cannot find the right words.

9.4 Practice

Very often we cannot find the right word for something. For example, take a ruler. If you did not know the name for it, you could ask someone:

What do you call that thing about 30 centimetres long made of plastic or wood? You use it to draw lines and measure things.

Make up more *'What do you call that thing . . .?'* questions about things you might find in a house or in a car or in an office.

9.5 Practice

Make a secret list of:

an electrical gadget	something you use in your job
something in your pocket or handbag	something you can eat
an item of clothing	

Describe the things in your list to another student. Do *not* say what the thing is called – let your partner work it out. If your first list turns out to be too easy, try making a more difficult one together with your partner and challenge the rest of the class.

9.6 Presentation: instructing people how to do things

There is not much difference between telling someone how something works and instructing them how to do it themselves. However, more detail is needed and more repetition, too. When giving instructions, we often link the steps together like this:

First of all you ...
The first thing you have to do is ...

After you've done that you ...
The next thing you do is ...

Oh, and by the way, don't forget to ...
Make sure you remember to ...
Oh, and be careful not to ...

The amount of detail and repetition usually depends on who you are talking to and how much they know already.
Decide how you would continue after using the expressions above.

9.7 Practice

Pick one of the gadgets you described in 9.5. Explain to your teacher how to use it. However, your teacher is going to pretend to be less mechanically-minded than he or she normally is. Your teacher is also going to play a number of different roles: an old lady, a child, a know-all, your boss.

9.8 Communication activity

Work in pairs. You will become an 'expert' on how to do something which you will have to explain carefully to your partner. One of you should look at activity 52, and the other at activity 104.

9.9 Presentation: checking understanding

If you are giving instructions to someone you will probably need to check as you go along that your listener understands, like this:

Alright so far?
Are you with me?
Is that clear?
Do you see what I mean?

And your listener may need encouragement if you are telling him or her how to do something. When you see your listener has understood you can say things like:

That's right. Now ...
Got that? Good! Now ...
Fine! Now ...

An encouraging tone of voice is very important if you want to sound helpful rather than superior. While you are *being given* complicated instructions, you may need to interrupt and ask questions like these:

Sorry, but I don't quite see why you have to ...
Sorry, can you say that again, please?
Sorry, but I'm not quite clear on ...

9.10 Communication activity

Work in pairs. There should be an even number of pairs divided into two groups, A and B. You will have to work out some instructions with your partner. The pairs in group A should all look at activity 51, and the pairs in group B at activity 82.

9.11 Practice

Make notes to prepare yourself to explain to the rest of the class (or large group):

1 How to get from the school to your home.
2 An activity connected with your hobby *or* your job. (Try to choose an activity which the others probably don't know much about.)

9.12 Written work

1 Write a description of an object or gadget as truthfully but as mysteriously as you can, so that your teacher can't guess what it is until you show him or her a picture or diagram of it.

Often notes and diagrams are a more effective visual presentation of instructions than sentence after sentence of detailed explanation. Discuss these ideas with your teacher before you start writing:

2 Use notes and diagrams to explain how to cook an egg the way you prefer.
3 Use notes and diagrams to show how to cook a national dish from your region or country.

10 Talking about similarities, talking about differences, stating preferences

10.1 Conversation

Jane: Hallo, Bob!
Bob: Hallo!
Jane: Oh, you've just left college, haven't you?
Bob: Yes.
Jane: What are you going to do?
Bob: Er... well, it... er... looks like a choice between teaching or... going into an office and...
Jane: Ah!
Bob: I think I'd much prefer to go in for teaching...
Jane: Jolly good!
Bob: Because... er... well, you get long holidays.
Jane: Mm.
Brenda: But, Bob, teachers' pay is nothing like as good as office pay.
Jane: Oh, Brenda, come on! It's... it used to be... teaching pay used to be very bad, but it's much improved now and I'm... I'm sure the two are fairly similar, actually.
Brenda: Really?
Jane: Mmmm!
Bob: Well, that's what I thought.
Jane: Oh, yes... yes.
Brenda: But I mean, wouldn't... wouldn't you get bored with the same routine year after year teaching... teaching the same material to children and...
Jane: And that's another thing! It wouldn't be anything like as boring as... as working in an office. Teaching is terribly stimulating. It's... it's new every day – I'm sure you'd enjoy it.
Brenda: But I mean, there's so much variety in office work! I mean, look at my job:

51

	I'm ... dealing with people and their problems, there's new situations to cope with all the time.
Jane:	Well ... maybe, but ... take responsibility: the ... the ... you don't need as great a sense of responsibility for your kind of work as you do in teaching – all those children, all those parents, not to mention the other teachers.
Brenda:	No, but you do have your ... your ... your colleagues at work – you have a certain amount of responsibility to *them*.
Jane:	Well, maybe they do have quite a lot in common after all – I don't know!
Brenda:	Oh, come off it! I think there's a tremendous number of differences between teaching and office work and, Bob, really it's just up to you to sort out which one you're going to enjoy doing more.
Bob:	Ah ... yes, well, I think I'll go for teaching because of the ... the long holidays – that really does attract me.
Jane:	Have you ... ever done any, actually?
Bob:	No, but it's fairly easy to pick up, isn't it?
Jane:	Oh, it's not as easy as it looks, you know!

10.2 Presentation: talking about similarities and slight differences

Look at these statistics:

	England	Scotland	Wales	Northern Ireland
Area (sq km)	130,441	78,775	20,768	14,120
Population	46,029,000	5,229,000	2,723,596	1,536,000
Highest mountain (height)	Scafell Pike 978m	Ben Nevis 1342m	Snowdon 1085m	Slieve Donard 852m
Largest city (population)	London 6,970,100	Glasgow 809,700	Cardiff 287,000	Belfast 363,000

We can point out the similarities between these countries like this:

In spite of the obvious differences in size and population, the countries of the UK have *quite a lot in common*.

Wales and Northern Ireland are *fairly similar* in size, though the area of Wales is *slightly* larger.

There *isn't much difference* in population between Cardiff and Belfast, though Belfast is *just a little* larger.

Scafell Pike and Snowdon are *more or less the same* height, though Snowdon is *just a few* metres higher.

Both Snowdon *and* Ben Nevis are over 1000 m high, though *neither* of them is *all that* high compared with the Alps, for example.

Neither Scotland *nor* Wales has *anything like as* many people as England.

Practise using similar sentences to make other comparisons between the four countries. Write your best sentences down. How is your own country similar to the countries listed?

10.3 Practice

In small groups, compare your own country with Britain (or with another country you know well). What are the *similarities*?

Climate	Food and drink
Industry	Attitude to women
People	Agriculture
Telephones	Political climate
Traffic	Television
Railways	Education
Scenery	Family life
City life	Clothes

Tell your partners about the similarities. Ask each other *'In what way?'* and *'How do you mean?'* questions.

10.4 Practice

In pairs or small groups, find a topic which is of mutual interest – you might like to talk about different cars, hi-fi systems, films, holiday resorts, cities or clothes, for example. Discuss the similarities between them. Report your discussion to the rest of the class.

10.5 Presentation: talking about differences

Look at these statistics:

	United Kingdom	Republic of Ireland
Area (sq km)	244,103	68,892
Population	55,515,000	2,978,248
Highest mountain (height)	Ben Nevis 1342m	Carrantuohill 1041m
Largest city (population)	London 6,970,100	Dublin 567,866

We can point out the differences between these countries like this:

In spite of the fact that they share a common language, Britain and Ireland have *very little in common*.

Ireland is *nothing like as* large as Britain – in fact, Ireland is about a quarter the size of Britain.

There are *nowhere near as* many people in Ireland as in Britain – in fact, the population of Britain is almost twenty times the size.

London is *a great deal* larger than Dublin – in fact, it's one of the largest cities in the world.

There are *a tremendous number of* differences between the people in Britain and the Irish – their attitudes, opinions and behaviour are *totally* different.

Point out the differences between your own country and Britain or Ireland in the same way. Write down your best sentences.

10.6 Practice

In large groups, comment on the differences between the countries shown in these statistics:

	USA	Canada	Australia	New Zealand	UK
Area (sq km)	9,363,404	9,975,223	7,704,441	268,675	244,103
Population	226,504,825	23,671,500	14,514,200	3,144,700	55,515,000
Highest mountain (height)	Mt McKinley 6,194m	Mt Logan 6,050m	Kosciusko 2,229m	Mt Cook 3,764m	Ben Nevis 1,342m
Largest city (population)	New York 17,557,288	Toronto 2,803,101	Sydney 3,193,300	Auckland 805,900	London 6,970,100

Report your discussion to the other group or groups. What are the differences between your own country and the countries you have been discussing?

10.7 Practice

In small groups, compare your own country with Britain (or with another country you know well) again. This time, what are the *differences*?

Climate	Public transport
People	Sport
Scenery	Language
Food	System of government
Family life	Weights and measurements
Standard of living	Prices
Licensing hours	Driving rules and habits
Breakfast	Houses

Tell your partners about the differences. Ask each other '*In what way?*' and '*How do you mean?*' questions.

10.8 Practice

Here are some ideas for a more general discussion. In small groups, talk about the differences and similarities between them:

A holiday in a hotel	*v.*	A camping holiday
Working in an office	*v.*	Working in a factory
Getting married	*v.*	Staying single
Life now	*v.*	Life ten years ago
Playing chess	*v.*	Playing cards
British food	*v.*	Your country's food
Learning English	*v.*	Learning your language

10.9 Practice

Team up with another student and talk about your family, job, education, experiences and interests. Try to find the similarities and differences between your life and your partner's life.
When you have enough information, change partners and report what you have found out to someone else.

10.10 Presentation: stating preferences

Comparing things often involves making a choice. If we are comparing different cars, for example, we often state our preferences at the same time. Here are some useful ways of stating what you prefer:

As far as I'm concerned, the best . . .
From my point of view, the best . . .
I'd go for this one because . . .
I'd much prefer that one because . . .
This one is preferable because . . .
I'd rather have that one because . . .

Decide how you would use these expressions to talk about different things to eat and drink. Perhaps look at a restaurant menu and decide what dishes to select.

10.11 Practice

Look at the map of Central Southern England on the next page. It gives information about three different places: Salisbury, Southampton and Swanage. In a group of three or four, decide which place would be best:

1 for a holiday
2 to work in
3 to visit for the day

Explain why. You can make this more exciting by acting as 'Publicity Officer' for one of the places.

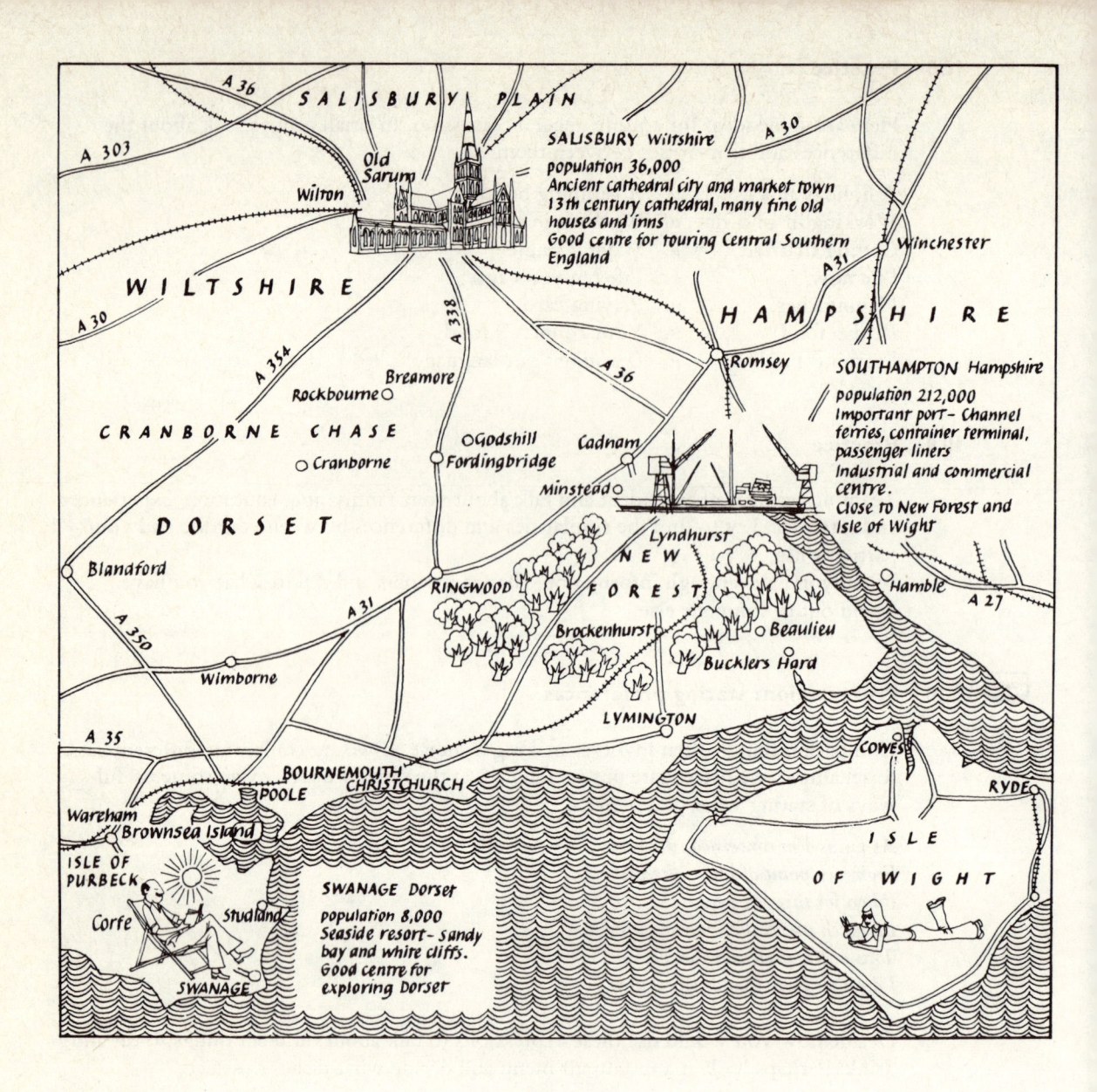

10.12 Practice

Look at the three job advertisements on the next page. Talk with another student about the similarities and differences and state your own preference. Decide what each job would involve – what sort of work, how much money, how much free time, how much worry, and so on.

If there is time, report your decisions back to the whole class.

STARLINE OF BLACKPOOL
require one SALESMAN
aged 33-55
✻ previous experience not necessary

This is a top-class selling/business job which will give you permanent, secure employment for the rest of your working life.

Starline are field leaders in the manufacture of sales ideas, business gifts, diaries and calendars which sell all year round to every type of trade and industry and have a repeat value of approximately 75 per cent.

Your success is guaranteed by our outstanding Sales Training Course and field help. Within a year your income can be £3,000 to £5,500 and, after the first four or five weeks, you will get a company car and other valuable fringe benefits.

Apply in writing, giving brief details of your career to date, to:
STARLINE (Sales Ideas) Ltd.,
Starline House, Mowbray Drive, Blackpool,
Lancashire FY3 7XB.
Tel. 0253-32126.

ANTARCTIC VOYAGE

CHIEF COOK
SECOND COOK AND BAKER
SECOND STEWARD
ASSISTANT STEWARD
CATERING BOYS

required on

ROYAL RESEARCH SHIP

Seven-month voyage including calls to United States and South America. Excellent salary and conditions. Long leave fully paid.

Apply in writing, giving full particulars of past working experience, to Catering Office, R.R.S. Bansfield, c/o Vosper Thornycroft Ltd., Northam Yard, Northam, Southampton, SO9 2VE.

WOOLCO
DEPARTMENT STORE
requires a PART-TIME
STORE DETECTIVE
(preferably female), with some experience, to complement their team. Part time, approx. 20 hours per week Monday to Saturday.

Please apply in writing to:
Mr. Skipsey,
Assistant General Manager,

WOOLCO
DEPARTMENT STORE
Castle Lane West
Bournemouth Tel 56201

10.13 Written work

Talk about these topics with your teacher before you start writing:

1 An English friend who has never left home before is coming to stay in your country. Write a letter telling him or her what will be different there.

2 Write a paragraph describing the similarities and differences between two British newspapers you have read.

3 Write an account of the similarities and differences between this book and the last book you learnt English from. Which do you prefer and why?

11 Making suggestions and giving advice, expressing enthusiasm, persuading

11.1 Conversation

Richard: Cigarette?
Jane: No, thank you. I've given up, you know.
Richard: Oh.
Jane: It's ten days ago. Haven't had one.
Richard: Well, you don't mind if I have one.
Jane: Well, alright, then... Oh my goodness! That's a terrible cough.
Richard: No, no, it's not. It's only... it's only... I only get it first thing in the morning.
Jane: That's going to make you very unfit, you know.
Richard: No, it's alright... it just... it goes in a minute... ah...
Jane: Why don't you try and give up?
Richard: Oh, no. I ought to, I can't. Relaxes me, smoking.
Jane: Really?
Richard: Mm, it does.
Jane: Well, have you ever thought of just cutting down?
Richard: Oh, no, that's all very well but... er... I wouldn't enjoy it. I depend a bit on my smoking, I must say.
Jane: You could do it gradually. I mean... well, if you tried... have you thought of just giving up one every day?
Richard: Yes, oh well, yes, that is quite a good idea...
Jane: It is?
Richard: ... but I think I'd lose count or something.

Jane: Oh dear! Well... well, it might be an idea if you started eating sweets.
Richard: Oh no, I couldn't do that... couldn't possibly...
Jane: Why?
Richard: Well, it makes you fat... sweets.
Jane: Well, do you think that matters? Don't you think it's better to be fat than to be unhealthy?
Richard: No, I don't. I'd rather be fat... I'd rather be thin than fat, certainly.
Jane: Oh dear, oh dear... well...
Richard: Anyway...
Jane: Hey! I've got a great idea!
Richard: What's that?
Jane: Why don't you go to a hypnotist? My sister did!
Richard: Oh... look, you don't seem to realize that... that I like smoking. If I gave it up, if I didn't smoke at all, I'd probably end up attacking people!
Jane: Oh, don't be so silly! Of course you wouldn't!

11.2 Presentation: making suggestions and giving advice

There are many ways of trying to get people to do things for their own good. The expressions you use depend on:
a) how difficult or unpleasant the course of action you suggest is.
b) who you are and who you are talking to – the roles you are playing and your relationship.

In this list the expressions are in order of tentativeness:

TENTATIVE *I was wondering if you'd ever thought of...*
Might it be an idea to...
Have you ever thought of...
Don't you think it might be an idea to...
You could always...
If I were you I'd...
Why don't you...
DIRECT *You'd better...*

Decide when you would use the different expressions. How would you continue after each one?

11.3 Practice

Your teacher is fed up with his or her present boring, unrewarding job. Suggest what he or she should do. Help your teacher with advice about evening, weekend and holiday plans, too.

11.4 Practice

Work in small groups. Each of you is returning home soon and you have to take presents for your father, mother, sister, brother, grandmother, grandfather, best friend, fiancé(e), niece, nephew etc. Ask for advice on what to take for each of them.

11.5 Practice

Work in groups. What advice would you give to the people who wrote the following letters to an advice column in a newspaper?

I have just lost my job at the age of 43. I have a wife and 6 children to support and there seems to be no chance of getting another job. We don't want to move to another area away from our friends and relations. The other problem is that I am in debt — I owe the bank £500. Can you give me any advice?

I am 25 years old and I have a super job in an advertising agency, working for a lovely boss. The prospects for promotion look really good, but before I get too old I want to see the world. What I dream of doing is taking a year off and hitch-hiking round the world alone. The problem is that my boss says he can't keep my job open for me. My boyfriend is against me going too — he says it's too dangerous. What do you think I should do?

I am a housewife and a friend has just told me that my husband, Jim, is having an affair with his secretary. I'm worried because he often comes home late and says he has been working late at the office. Last week-end he said he had to go away to Paris on business. I really don't know what to do; our two daughters are still at school and I don't want Jim to leave us. I just don't know what to do.

I am 55 years old and a bachelor. Now after all these years I have fallen desperately in love. The girl I love is much younger than me — in fact she's 20 years old. She says she loves me but my relations say she is just after my money. Her parents don't approve of me and want her to forget me. I don't want to be lonely for the rest of my life. What should I do?

When you have decided on what advice to give, report back to the rest of the class.

11.6 Communication activity

Work in groups of four. Each of you will be offering advice to different people on their personal problems. Student A should look at activity 43, student B at activity 33, student C at activity 83 and student D at activity 5.

11.7 Presentation: expressing enthusiasm

When we give advice, we often need to 'sell' our ideas. A natural salesman can use the 'soft sell' approach and sell his product without putting any pressure on the customer. But most people have to show a lot of enthusiasm when they are trying to 'sell' a product or an idea.

When we are enthusiastic we use adjectives like these:

magnificent *amazing*
terrific *incredible*
fantastic *great*

They are often put into introductory phrases like these:

I think it'd be a fantastic idea to . . .
I've got a terrific idea: . . .
Listen! This'd be great . . .
Hey! I've got this amazing idea: . . .

Decide how you would continue from these phrases. Practise your 'enthusiastic' tone of voice, too!

11.8 Practice

Begin in pairs and work out some ideas on each of these topics:

What to do next lesson
A good book to read
A good record to listen to
A good film to see
How to practise English out of school
How to become rich

When you are ready, make enthusiastic suggestions to the rest of the class.

11.9 Communication activity

Work in groups of three. You will be discussing plans for the weekend. Student A should look at activity 13, student B at activity 119 and student C at activity 77.

11.10 Presentation: persuading

People do not always just accept suggestions and advice, they say things like this:

That's all very well, but ...
That's easier said than done, you see ...
You don't seem to realize that ...
That's quite a good idea, but ...

And then they state their doubts or objections. They may then need persuading. You can often answer objections with phrases like these:

I see what you mean, but if ...
That's true, but if ...

Decide how you would continue these openings if someone suggested, for example, climbing Mount Everest.

11.11 Practice

Your teacher smokes and drinks and eats too much. Persuade him or her to stop or cut down and suggest some possible methods.

11.12 Communication activity

Work in pairs. Each person has different holiday plans. One of you should look at activity 141, and the other at activity 94.

11.13 Communication activity

Work in groups of four. Each person has seen a different magazine advertisement. Student A should look at activity 72, student B at activity 29, student C at activity 4 and student D at activity 117.

11.14 Practice

Tell the rest of the class (or group) about a matter you'd really like some advice on. Ask them to help you solve your problem. Don't accept all their suggestions – let yourself be persuaded!

11.15 Written work

Here are extracts from three letters you have received. Discuss them with your teacher before replying to them:

> There's this very important exam coming up soon and I've simply got to pass. The trouble is I can't seem to get down to studying. There are so many distractions and there's not much time left.
> I hope you can help,
> Robert.

> looking for some ideas on how to celebrate their silver wedding. We've got about £100 to spend and we want to do something that'll be really memorable. Have you got any ideas? Please let me know
> Regards,
> Richard

> in fact I'm at my wit's end. He left two days ago and I'm sure he isn't coming back. He mentioned something about leaving the country and I'm afraid he may have got mixed up in a crime or something. I can't go to the police in case he gets into trouble. What shall I do?
> Please write soon,
> love,
> Susan.

12 Complaining, apologizing and forgiving, expressing disappointment

12.1 Conversation

Brenda: Morning, Bob! Late again!
Bob: Oh, I'm ever so sorry. I can't tell you how sorry I am.
Brenda: Mm... what's the excuse this time?
Bob: Ah... I just don't know what to say. I must have turned the alarm clock off and gone back to sleep again, I...
Brenda: Yeah, and last week one of the children wasn't well?
Bob: Yes, I know...
Brenda: Mmm!
Bob: ... I'm really sorry, I promise you it won't happen again.
Brenda: Never mind! Look, I've got a bit... bit of a problem here, you see Buxton's phoned while you were out.
Bob: Yes.
Brenda: And I just don't know anything about what's going on there, so I told them that you were in a meeting and that you'd call them as soon as you got back.
Bob: Oh, OK. Right, thanks very much.
Brenda: And... er... oh... er, um, er... I'm not quite sure how to put this, but a meeting's been called for this evening at 6 o'clock and I can't go.
Bob: Oh, that's alright, don't worry. I'll... Oh! This evening?
Brenda: Yeah.
Bob: Oh, I'd arranged to go out... er... yeah... oh well, never mind, it doesn't really matter. Yeah, OK, I'll cover the meeting. Don't worry, I'll make up for...
Brenda: Are you sure?
Bob: ... being late a couple of times. Yes, yes.
Brenda: Fine, thanks.

Bob: Er... now, what's this?... Er... oh dear! Bad news I'm afraid. We'll have to postpone the staff outing. The... er... theatre have sent our cheque back – they couldn't supply tickets for the night we wanted to go to see the show.
Brenda: Oh no! I was really looking forward to that.
Bob: Well, still it can't be helped.
Brenda: Oh, it's such a pity!
Bob: Oh, well, not to worry, I suppose. Er... we'll have to get together and... er... fix up another date that everybody can manage – say about three or four weeks' time and then we can... er... go and see the play then.
Brenda: We should have booked earlier!
Bob: Yes, well, can't win them all. That's life!
Brenda: I'm really disappointed. That was something I wanted to see so much.
Bob: Well, never mind!

12.2 Presentation: complaining

A direct complaint in English often sounds very rude indeed. To be polite we usually 'break it gently' and use expressions like these before we actually come to the point:

I wonder if you could help me...
Look, I'm sorry to trouble you, but...
I've got a bit of a problem here, you see...
I'm sorry to have to say this, but...

It is usually better to break it gently like this than to say, for example:

Look here! I wish you'd arrive on time.
OR *I've just about had enough of your unpunctuality.*

It is often not enough to just say '*Sorry*' and promise it won't happen again. You may need to apologize more profusely, like this:

Oh dear, I'm most awfully sorry.
I can't tell you how sorry I am.
I'm so sorry, I didn't realize.
I just don't know what to say.
I'm ever so sorry.

Decide how you would use these expressions, for example, in conversations between a teacher and a student.

12.3 Practice

You are staying in a hotel and a lot of things have gone wrong. Build conversations like this from the prompts below, using the expressions presented in 12.2:

Guest: Excuse me, I wonder if you can help me.
Manager: What seems to be the trouble, sir?
Guest: Well, you see, there doesn't seem to be any hot water in my room.
Manager: Oh, I'm sorry. I'll have it seen to at once.
Guest: Thanks very much.

hot water	soup
heating	steak
pillows	coffee
TV	no ice
draught	slow service

12.4 Communication activity

Work in two groups. You will be playing the roles of shopkeepers and customers. Group A should look at activity 60, group B at activity 6.

12.5 Communication activity

Work in pairs. You will be playing the roles of neighbours and friends, so make sure you are polite. Remember that neighbours and friends can get very upset by complaints and criticism. One of you should look at activity 128, and the other at activity 54. You will find it more convenient to stand up, so that you can approach your partner and then walk away after each conversation.

12.6 Presentation: apologizing and forgiving

When you do something wrong, you can save yourself a lot of trouble by apologizing first – before someone complains to you. In this case it may be even more essential to 'break it gently' in English. Here are some useful opening expressions:

I'm not quite sure how to put this, but . . .
I've got a bit of an apology to make, you see . . .
I'm afraid I've got something to tell you . . .
Um, this isn't easy to explain, but . . .
I've got a confession to make . . .

After someone has heard what you've done they may ask you to explain how it happened. They may then forgive you, if you're lucky, like this:

Oh, that's alright, don't worry.
It's not really your fault.
Please don't blame yourself.
Oh, never mind, it doesn't really matter.

Decide how you would use these expressions if, for example, you took your friend's dog out for a walk and it ran away.

12.7 Practice

Build conversations like this from the prompts below, using the expressions presented in 12.6:

A: I'm not quite sure how to put this, but you know that hair-dryer you lent me.
B: Yes.
A: Well, I'm afraid I somehow dropped it on the floor and it doesn't seem to work any more.
B: Oh, that's alright, don't worry – it hasn't been working properly for ages.

transistor radio	electric kettle
slide projector	alarm clock
tape recorder	lawn mower
electric mixer	tennis racket
vacuum cleaner	dictionary

12.8 Communication activity

Work in pairs. You will be playing the roles of friends, then boss and assistant. One of you should look at activity 67, and the other at activity 36.

12.9 Presentation: expressing disappointment

Sometimes unpleasant things happen which can't be blamed on anyone. But we may want to express our disappointment to others. Here are some useful ways of doing this:

I was really looking forward to ...
It really is a shame that ...
It's such a pity that ...
I'm really disappointed that ...
If only ...
I wish ...

Often disappointments have to be taken philosophically – we can't let things upset us too much. Here are some ways of reacting calmly and changing the subject:

Still, it can't be helped.
Still, it's nothing to worry about, I suppose.
Well, it's no good crying over spilt milk.
Well, you can't win them all.
That's life.
Oh well, not to worry, I suppose.

Decide how you would use these expressions if, for example, bad weather had prevented you from going out for a picnic.

12.10 Practice

Build conversations like this about the situations below, using the expressions presented in 12.9.

A: I was really looking forward to the match.
B: Yes, so was I. If only it hadn't rained so much in the night. It would've been a really exciting game.
A: Still, it can't be helped.
B: No, I suppose not. What shall we do instead?
A: Well, we could ...

1 Football match cancelled because of rain.
2 Theatre has 'House full' sign outside.
3 In a restaurant the first course was so big you couldn't eat the main course you both ordered.
4 You missed the party because you were ill.
5 Your car is at the garage – you can't go on the trip.

6 What you had at the restaurant was bad – what the others had looked delicious.
7 You had a headache, so you didn't enjoy the concert.
8 You were both on holiday and forgot your address books, so you couldn't send anyone a card.

12.11 Communication activity

Work in groups of three. Each of you has some bad news for your friends. Student A should look at activity 148, student B at activity 21 and student C at activity 62.

12.12 Communication activity

Work in pairs. You will be playing the roles of student and housewife. One of you should look at activity 96, and the other at activity 86.

12.13 Written work

Discuss these ideas with your teacher before you write these letters:

1 You bought a cheap radio-cassette player by mail order last year and now it's gone wrong. Write a letter to the company you bought it from.

2 You stayed at a terrible hotel for two weeks as part of a package tour. Write a letter to the tour operator complaining about the various things that went wrong. Ask for a refund.

3 Your friend has failed his university final exams. Write a letter to sympathize.

13 Describing places, describing people

13.1 Conversation

Jane: Bob, could you do me a real favour, please?
Bob: Yes, of course.
Jane: I've arranged to meet this friend, Tony, tomorrow at one o'clock and I'm going to be late ... er ... I can't ring him because he's not on the phone ...
Bob: Yes.
Jane: ... so I wondered if you could go along and meet him for me. Would that be alright?
Bob: Oh yes, yes certainly.
Jane: Oh, thank you very much.
Bob: Um ... you'd better tell me what he looks like.
Jane: Yes, of course, you've never seen him, have you? Um ... well, he's ... average height and build. Um ... sort of fairish with ...
Bob: Yes.
Jane: ... with blue eyes, I think ... um ...
Bob: Average? What, about five foot ten?
Jane: Mm ... yes, I suppose so.
Bob: Yes ... and does he ... erm ... wear glasses or anything like that?
Jane: No, he doesn't. No, but he's got a moustache. He's got a sort of blond ... blondy moustache.
Bob: Uhhu.
Jane: Um ... he'll be quite sloppily dressed, you know ...
Bob: Yes.
Jane: ... jeans and a tee-shirt hanging out or something. Oh, I know how you can recognize him – he's always smiling!

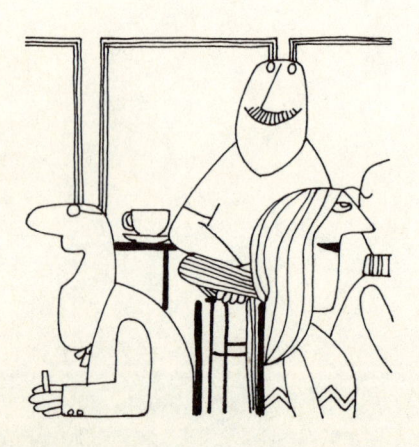

Bob: Oh, right, right.
Jane: So just look for someone like that.
Bob: Er...um...where...where do you want me to meet him?
Jane: Ah yes, well, it's a place called...a little tea place in a place called...Sorry, I'm being terribly muddling for you, aren't I? It's a place called Neal's Yard.
Bob: Yes.
Jane: ...and it's a little tea shop and he'll be upstairs.
Bob: Right...how...how do you get to this Neal's Yard place?
Jane: You don't know it? Er...go to Covent Garden tube station.
Bob: Yes.
Jane: And when you come out, you walk straight up Neal Street.
Bob: Yes.
Jane: And then it's the...one, two, three...third on the left...
Bob: Right.
Jane: ...and it's lovely, it's a tiny little street...er...very narrow – cobbles.
Bob: Yes.
Jane: And then you go along that and it opens up into a very pretty yard.
Bob: Um...what kind of place is it? I mean...
Jane: Well, it used to be warehouses...
Bob: Yes.
Jane: ...and most of them have been converted into offices or...or shops. And this is in one corner...um...just go in and up the stairs and he'll be there and it...it's lovely because it's all wood panelling and so on and you can...
Bob: So there'll be quite a few people around?
Jane: Oh yes, yes, and...
Bob: But I should be able to recognize him quite easily?
Jane: Oh, I should think so, yes.
Bob: Oh...um...er...what's...er...what is he interested in? I mean, what are we going to talk about for half an hour or so?
Jane: Oh, that's no problem...no problem, actually, because...er...he plays tennis – just like you.
Bob: Ah!
Jane: So there you are!
Bob: Right!
Jane: And he's married with children, so you can talk about that, as well.
Bob: OK.
Jane: And I'll get there as quickly as I can!
Bob: Fine.

13.2 Presentation: describing places

You often have to describe places to people – a house or building they haven't seen, a town or city or village they haven't visited, scenery or countryside they aren't familiar with and so on. Here are some of the questions you may have to answer:

Where is it?
What does it look like?
How do you get there?
What's interesting or remarkable about it?
What's pleasant or unpleasant about it?

If it's a house or a building you may also have to answer questions like these:

What other buildings are around it?
What's it used for?
How old is it?

Decide how you would answer these questions to talk about:

The building you're in now and the buildings nearby
The town you're in now
The countryside near the town you're in now

13.3 Practice

Look at the pictures below. Imagine they are postcards you sent while you were on holiday. With your teacher's help, make a list of the words you need to describe each place and then give a description with as much detail as possible.

13.4 Practice

Work alone first and make a secret list of:

A well-known building
A town or city you know
A local landmark
A well-known street or road
An area or country you know

Then work in small groups and *without* saying *where* each place is, describe it to your partners. Get them to guess the name of the place after you have described it.

13.5 Practice

Get together with two or three others and describe your favourite place to them. Try to make it sound as attractive as possible!

13.6 Presentation: describing people

You often have to answer this question: *'What's so and so like?'*
This does not usually mean giving a detailed description of a person's physical appearance. A better way to answer the question is to say what sort of person he or she is, to mention some striking characteristics and perhaps give an assessment of his or her character.
So here are some of the characteristics you may use to describe someone:

General personal impression
Age
Height, weight, build or figure
Face, hair, eyes, complexion . . .
Clothes
Character
Interests, sports and hobbies
Job
Their life so far: achievements, family background, . . .

Think about various people you know and decide how you would describe them. Find out the words you need by asking other members of the class or your teacher, or using a dictionary.

13.7 Practice

Look at the people in the pictures on page 74 and on the front cover of the book. How would you describe each of the people in the pictures?

13.8 Practice

Look at everyone in the room very carefully for a couple of minutes. Then stand back to back with one of them and, *without looking*, describe each other. Keep going until everyone has had a turn.

13.9 Practice

Work alone for a few minutes and make a secret list of:

A male film-star
A female film-star
A famous singer
A well-known politician
Another teacher
Another student
Someone nobody else in the class knows

When you are ready, work in small groups and get the others to ask you questions to find out who you have in mind. Avoid answering questions which will allow the others to guess the name of the person too quickly.

13.10 Practice

Begin by closing your eyes and try to visualize:

Your home and town
The members of your family
The people you work with
Your friends

After a few minutes' silence, get together with two or three other students and describe to them the main characteristics of these places and people. Find out as much as possible about *their* homes and the people *they* know – try to form a clear visual impression of everything and everyone they describe.

Report one of your partners' most interesting or vivid descriptions to the rest of the class.

13.11 Written work

Discuss these ideas with your teacher before you start writing:

1 Your teacher is arriving at the airport but you cannot meet the plane yourself. Write a description of him or her so that someone else can go to meet the plane and will be able to recognize him or her.

2 You have arranged to meet someone at a friend's house. Unfortunately, you can only remember the name of the road, not the number of the house. Write a description of the house so that your friend can find it.

3 Cut a photograph of two or more people from a magazine or newspaper. Write a description of them and where they are.

14 Telling a story: narrative techniques, handling dialogue, controlling a narrative

14.1 Conversation

Tony: Did I ever tell you about the ... time that I moved to Ireland with my family?
Leo: No.
Tony: Well, my father was still ... learning to drive a car at the time ... er ... so he wasn't feeling too confident ... [Mm] when the ... the ferry docked in Belfast and the car was unloaded. Anyway, we set off and ... er ... haha ... he became more and more uncomfortable because ... well, what happened was ... er ... everywhere we went, people started to point at the car and laugh. Well, my dad was getting more and more agitated really. You can guess ... how he felt, trying to drive in a ... in a strange city when he ... wasn't too sure what he was doing or ... or where he was going ... [Mm] or indeed why everyone was laughing at him. He wanted to know what the fuss was all about, so ... eventually he stopped the car ... er ... got out and spoke to a group of women who were standing on the pavement and asked them just what was so amusing. Well, the explanation was really quite simple ... um ... at that time they didn't have a ... a driving test in Ireland. [Oh!] So no one was used to seeing L plates ... [Haha!] stuck all over a car – foreigners and their ... and their funny ways, you see. [Yeah ... yeah] So, well, to cut a long story short, my dad went straight down to the post office and bought himself a driving licence.
Leo: *Bought* himself a driving licence?
Tony: Yes. I mean, you could just pay the money over the counter and walk away with a licence.

Leo: Good heavens!
Tony: And ... er ... he never has taken a test – he's seventy-three now ... [Mm] he's still happily driving his car. [Yeah] Mind you, he's never ... he's never been a very good driver!
Leo: Haha.
Tony: Haha.

14.2 Presentation: narrative techniques

We often want to tell people stories in the form of long narratives. It may be the story of a film or a book, for example, or a true story of events that have happened to us – or even a joke or funny story.

To keep the narrative going you need various 'narrative techniques' to give variety and interest to the story. One useful narrative technique is to create suspense by making the listener wait for important information. So instead of saying:

He fell into the sea.

you can say:

What happened to him was that he fell into the sea.

And instead of saying:

He opened the letter.

you can say:

What he did was open the letter.

or even:

What happened was that he opened the letter.

Another technique is to involve the listener in the story by asking him or her to guess what happened next or how someone in the story felt.

You can guess how he felt.
What do you think he did?
And then do you know what he did?
Imagine my surprise when he ...
You'll never guess what happened next.

Narrative techniques like these will help make a story more dramatic. Think of more examples and decide when you could use them in telling a simple story everyone knows.

14.3 Practice

Look at the strip cartoon on page 80. Decide together how you would tell the story, using the techniques presented in 14.2.

14.4 Communication activity

Work in pairs. You will tell each other a story in your own words. One of you should look at activity 135, and the other at activity 87.

14.5 Practice

Work in groups. Make a secret note of the titles of two films you have seen – one really good and the other really bad – and two novels you have read – one good and one bad.
Tell the others in the group the story of each. See if they can guess the title when you have finished.

14.6 Presentation: handling dialogue

In a narrative you can choose whether to report things people said like this:

He told me to leave.

or like this:

He said, 'If you don't get out of here this minute, I'll call the police.'

The first way is good if you only want to report the main point of what was said. The second way is good if you want to report exactly what was said.

Here are some other ways of reporting the main point of what was said:

He wanted to know . . .
He wondered . . .
He tried to find out . . .
He went on to say that . . .
He mentioned something about . . .
He hinted that . . .
I found out that . . .

Decide how you would continue these opening phrases. Think of several examples.

14.7 Communication activity

Work in pairs. Each of you will have a story to put into dialogue form (you will have to do some writing, so make sure you have some paper). One of you should look at activity 46, and the other at activity 111.

14.8 Presentation: controlling a narrative

You can signal the beginning of a spoken personal narrative like this:

Did I ever tell you about the time I . . .
That reminds me of the time I . . .
Funny you should mention that, because something similar happened to me once . . .
That's funny, because something similar happened to a friend of mine once . . .

A story often has changes of direction and digressions. You can signal the end of a digression like this:

Anyway, . . .
As I was saying, . . .
To get back to the story, . . .

And we can speed up the end of a story by cutting out irrelevant detail and saying:

To cut a long story short . . .
Anyway, what happened in the end was . . .

Decide how you would use these expressions if, for example, you were telling the story in the strip cartoon on the next page.

14.9 Communication activity

Work in pairs. Each of you will have a story to retell in your own words. One of you should look at activity 140, and the other at activity 149.

The Silent Three
OFF THE DEEP END
On hot afternoons, Jocasta Wright, (an art student), & Belinda Weber (taking A Levels in French & Spanish), frequent swimming baths....
Jocasta
Belinda
Jocasta SWIMS:
I'm a STRONG swimmer - I LOVE being out of my DEPTH...
Belinda sunbathes:
I can't SWIM... I HATE getting my HAIR wet and my MASCARA runs & the CHLORINE makes my eyes all RED.
Whilst Jocasta disports herself in the pool.......
...Belinda lies blissfully:
And she does LIE too! Belinda's always telling MEN she's an ACTRESS ...or a COURIER....
..or, sometimes, she pretends to be FRENCH: "Ai dunt spik Eengleesh ver waal." THAT really turns the blokes on!
But what really BUGS me - she always pretends to be THICK...she thinks it's ATTRACTIVE...never lets on she's INTELLIGENT...always COOING and SIMPERING. ARTIFICIALLY DUMB blondes make me want to THROW-UP!
Today, Belinda is a MODEL....
Yeah, I've just been doing a modelling job in Martinique
My left foot!
All over tan, eh?
But just after she got back from Martinique, she began taking 2 A Levels...& she's got 8 O-Levels...& she's probably going to university....
and they say her translations of Heberto Padilla are highly competent...
You COW, Jocasta! I don't want them to know I'm a SWOT! ..it's so UNSEXY.
I just think it's time you learnt to SWIM....
..otherwise you'll spend your whole life in the SHALLOW END.
© Posy Simmonds 1978

14.10 Practice

Work in small groups. Help each other to remember:

An unforgettable evening
An embarrassing experience
A frightening experience
An experience which made you laugh
A dream you remember
A joke or funny story

Listen to each other's narratives, but don't interrupt except to find out more details.

14.11 Practice

Sit in a circle. Every alternate person is A and the person on his or her right is B. If you are A, tell the person on your right a story, an experience, a joke or a funny story. If you are B, listen to the story from the person on your left and tell it to the person on your right. And so on round the class until the story comes back to the person who told it first.

Was the story you told recognizable on its return? Tell the others how it had changed.

Then it's B's turn to tell a story to the person on his or her right. And so on round the circle.

14.12 Written work

1 Write a letter to a friend, describing one of the experiences you talked about during this unit. Tell the story as if it happened quite recently.

2 Look at these newspaper headlines. First, discuss with your teacher what sort of story would have followed each headline:

ORDEAL OF HIJACK HOSTAGES
HOLIDAY RUINED FOR TOURISTS
ARCHBISHOP ON DRINKS CHARGE
50 GIRLS TAKEN ILL ON BUS
FIREMEN STARTED FIRES
'GHOST' SEEN IN CINEMA
POLICEMAN SENT TO PRISON

Choose one or two and write *both* the newspaper report that followed the headline *and* a personal report by one of the participants. Discuss with your teacher how the *style* of each report would be different – perhaps look at an English newspaper first.

15 Dealing with moods and feelings: anger, sadness, indifference. Saying goodbye

15.1 Conversation

Bob: Jenny, I'm sorry to keep you waiting! I've just about had enough of it! I parked my car outside a newsagent's for a couple of minutes to go in and get a paper and a magazine and some chocolate for the journey, and this bloody traffic warden stuck a parking ticket on my windscreen!
Jenny: Ohh! Rotten luck!
Bob: I mean, you know, these damn little 'wasps' flitting around... I... Oh!
Jenny: Hey, don't get too upset. You're overreacting a bit, you know.
Bob: Well, why the hell should we have to put up with it? There's the poor motorist gets...
Liz: Hallo, you two!
Jenny: OK. Take it easy! Hallo, Liz. How are you today?
Bob: Hi!
Liz: Oh God! I just don't know what to do!
Bob: What's the matter?
Jenny: Why?
Liz: Well, you know that job I went for today – I lost it!
Jenny: Ohh!
Liz: It's the tenth job! I've been up for all these jobs.
Jenny: Rotten luck!
Bob: Oh, come on! It can't be as bad as all that.
Liz: Oh, honestly, Bob, that's what I really wanted, that job. And some little twit got – well, I mean, I don't know she was a twit. Maybe she's not.
Bob: Well, cheer up. Something'll come up.
Jenny: Try and look on the bright side. Maybe there's something better round the corner.
Liz: Oh, I know but it's very hard at the moment to do that!
Bob: You'll find something you really want to do.
Liz: Yeah, I know, but honestly now we're... splitting up I've got nobody to sort of tell my troubles to... couldn't have happened at a worse time.
Jenny: Oh, it's not as bad as all that, surely?
Bob: Got plenty of other friends, surely? I mean, you know...
Jenny: Hey, look! Why don't we have a reunion in about a year's time?
Liz: OK! That's a good idea!
Bob: What, a year from today?
Jenny: Yeah, why not?
Richard: Hallo, you lot!
Bob: That sounds...
Liz: Hi!
Jenny: How are you?

82

Bob: Hallo, Richard!
Richard: I'm alright, thanks.
Jenny: I was just saying, why don't we have a reunion in a year's time?
Richard: What for?
Jenny: For fun!!
Bob: So we can all meet up again ... and ... and ...
Liz: Yeah ... what do you think? Good idea?
Richard: What's the point?
Bob: Well! I mean you know ...
Liz: Well! ... doesn't have to be a point ... just for ...
Bob: ... we're good friends and ... er ... I'm going to miss you. I'm going away to Canada and ... er ... for a year. I'm going to miss you. I ... I want to see you when I come back!
Richard: Well, it's ... it's ... all a bit ... bit boring, isn't it?
Bob: Oh!
Jenny: I'm surprised you feel that way about it. I'd say it would be very nice to meet up in a year's time.
Bob: Yes!
Liz: It'll be interesting to see where we've got to and what things have happened to us.
Richard: Alright. Alright, yeah! Why not?
Jenny: Oh, that's good. Well, I'm glad that's settled.
Bob: Oh that's ... same time, same place next year.
Jenny: Er ... talking of time, look, I think ... er ...
Liz: Oh God, I must go too.
Bob: Oh, yes ... Well ...
Jenny: Anyway ...
Bob: Remember me to your parents. Hope to see them when I come back ...
Liz: Oh, good luck with your thing, Jenny! I hope it goes well.
Jenny: Thanks.
Richard: Well, if you're ever in Luton ... um ... come and see me – you've got the address. Got the address?
Liz: Yeah.
Bob: Really nice to know you all. I'm going to miss your friendship.
Jenny: Don't forget to drop me a line, will you?
Bob: Oh, I won't forget at all.
Liz: Right ...

Bob: Well...
Richard: See you then!
Jenny: OK. Good luck!
Richard: Goodbye! All the best!
Bob: Alright, bye!

15.2 Presentation: anger

It isn't always easy for us to keep our tempers when things go wrong. There are different degrees of anger and different ways of showing it.
Expressions like the following express annoyance:

What a nuisance!
That's typical!
That's just what I needed!
Good grief!

If we are in a bad mood, we sometimes get sarcastic and say things like this:

That's charming, that is!
That's wonderful!
That's absolutely great!
It was very nice of him to...

When we are more angry, we sometimes use swear words like these:

Damn!
Hell!
Bloody hell!
(More obscene expressions should be avoided because they may offend a lot of people.)

And if we are absolutely furious we are more likely to lose our tempers completely and say:

I've just about had enough of...
What a stupid bloody idiot!
Why the hell don't they...
It makes me sick the way they...
It makes my blood boil when this sort of thing happens!

One way to deal with someone who is angry is to try and calm them down by saying:

Take it easy!
Don't you think you're over-reacting a bit?
There's no need to get so upset.
It's not as bad as all that.
I'm sorry to hear that.

Decide how you would deal with different people's anger in some different situations. What would you say if they were angry with *you*?

84

15.3 Practice

Make a list of some of the things which have happened to you which really made you angry.
Imagine they have all happened today. Tell everyone about them angrily and let the others try to calm you down.

15.4 Communication activity

Work in pairs. In each situation, one of you will be angry and the other one has to calm you down. One of you should look at activity 115, the other at activity 42.

15.5 Presentation: sadness

We cannot always be bright and happy – sometimes we have moods of depression or sadness. Here are some ways of talking about how we feel:

Oh God! I just don't know what to do . . .
I can't take much more of this . . .
And as if that wasn't enough . . .
It's just been one of those days . . .

To help us out of our depression, we may need a sympathetic ear – someone to listen and cheer us up. Here are some ways of cheering people up:

Come on! It can't be as bad as all that . . .
Try and look on the bright side . . .
Cheer up!
Hey look, why don't we . . .

But it will probably make things worse if you say:

Snap out of it!
Don't be such a misery!
Pull yourself together!

15.6 Communication activity

Work in pairs. One person will be unhappy, while the other tries to be sympathetic. One of you should look at activity 103, the other at activity 59.

15.7 Communication activity

Work in pairs. One person will be happy, the other sad about some different things which have happened. One of you should look at activity 121, the other at activity 49.

15.8 Presentation: indifference

When we don't care one way or the other about something, we can be really boring and say:

I couldn't care less.
Please yourself.
What's the point?
I don't mind what you do.
The whole thing bores me to death.
It doesn't matter to me.
It's a bore, as far as I'm concerned.

It won't help if you react like this:

Don't be so boring!
What a misery you are!
You're a pain in the neck!
That's typical of you!

The best way to make someone take an interest is probably to try and point out the advantages of the idea or to interest them in a different idea. You can say things like this:

It's not as bad as all that, surely?
I'm surprised you feel that way about it.
Listen, if you look at it this way . . .
Oh, come on, it's actually quite interesting.
I see what you mean, but on the other hand . . .

Decide what you would say to interest someone in some different plans.

15.9 Communication activity

Work in pairs. Each of you will be pretending to be indifferent to each other's plans. One of you should look at activity 153, the other at activity 55.

15.10 Practice

The class is divided into four groups. Each group is in a different mood.
Group A: You are all in a bad temper.
Group B: You are all depressed.
Group C: You are all in a good mood.
Group D: You are all bored and indifferent.

When each group has established its mood by talking together, everyone goes round the class talking to different people. Try to make the people you meet share your mood!

At the end, tell everyone what you did and how successful you were. Did anyone manage to change your mood?

15.11 Presentation: saying goodbye

Well, the time has come for us to say goodbye.... If you're hoping to meet someone again soon, it's enough to say:

Bye for now!
See you!
Cheerio!
See you next week!
Have a good weekend!

But if it's goodbye for a long time (or for ever) you are more likely to say:

I've come to say goodbye.
Thanks for everything!

and:
Keep in touch!
Don't forget to give me a ring!
Remember to drop me a line!
If you're ever in ..., do come and see me – you've got my address.

and:
I'm really going to miss you, you know.
It's been really nice to know you.

and:
All the best.
Good luck with your...
I hope everything goes well.
Take care!
See you sometime soon, I hope.
Well, I'd better be going, I suppose.

15.12 Practice

Stand up and go round the class saying goodbye to everyone in the room, including your teacher. Imagine you're not going to see any of them again for a long time – perhaps never again.

15.13 Communication activity

Look at activity 45 before you finish this unit.

15.14 Written work

As this is the last unit, you probably don't feel like writing much. So here is just one suggestion:

Write a short report on what you have learnt from this book. What seem to be its strong and weak points?

Communication activities

1 In this part of the activity you are playing the role of stranger. Remain seated, some people will come to you for help with their problems.
Here is some information about your role, which may influence whether you agree to or refuse their requests. Remember that if you refuse you must be *polite* and give a good reason for refusing.

1 Your pen doesn't work very well.
2 You are in a part of town you don't know.
3 Your watch is unreliable – sometimes it's fast, sometimes it's slow.
4 You enjoy explaining English words to foreigners.
5 Your doctor has told you not to lift heavy weights.
6 You have just opened the window.
7 Your mother likes chocolates.
8 You don't smoke.

Someone will tell you what to do when you have finished.

---

2 Your friend, C, has taken over the organization of a picnic in the country for your class. C is going to give everyone jobs to do. You don't mind C organizing it but you feel the party shouldn't be too elaborate. On the other hand you realize that C can't do everything by himself or herself, so you should try to help in some way.

When you have finished, discuss the differences between the three parts of this activity.

---

3 Your group is planning to sail round the world in a yacht. You need to be as well-equipped as possible without spending too much money.
Decide what equipment, clothes etc. you are going to take and tell the rest of the class. If you disagree about an item, report it as a possible or probable item for inclusion. Give reasons why you need or don't need each item.
You are definitely going on this voyage, by the way – so don't spend time deciding if it's a good idea to go or not!

✓ = Yes, definitely
✓? = Yes, probably
?? = Perhaps
✗? = No, probably not
✗ = No, definitely not

4 You have cut this advertisement out of a newspaper. The product advertised seems really good – incredible value in fact. Persuade your partners to spend their money on this:

SWISS DIGITAL CHRONOGRAPH AND ANALOGUE WATCH. TWENTY EIGHT FUNCTIONS FOR ONLY £89.95. (+p&p)

Where but from Switzerland would you expect to find the finest combination of quartz chronograph technology married to the most beautiful of analogue alarm watches in one elegant stylish piece? Who but Scotcade could offer you a remarkable 28 functions for only £89.95.

Made by Buler, part of the foremost watchmaking group in Switzerland, the elegance and precision of this watch, set in a solid stainless steel bracelet, make it almost a piece of jewellery.

Why a two-faced watch?
Because with it you get the best of both worlds.
First, you get an analogue watch operated by a quartz chip which tells you the time so accurately it would seem the Greenwich Time signal could rely on it. Swiss craftsmanship ensures it is accurate to within a mere sixty seconds a year.

Beneath it is one of the most advanced digital chronographs made in Switzerland, with many functions on its liquid crystal display (LCD) the common chronograph just doesn't possess.

Multi-time zone.
A special function which enables you to tell the time in two places at once. For the travelling businessman who needs to know the time in both London and, say, Hong Kong, or for the holidaymaker simply going to Italy. You can programme two time zones which will be permanently recorded until you change them.

The Stopwatch.
At the touch of a button your Swiss watch turns into a sophisticated stopwatch for all those occasions when you need precision timing. Accurate to 100th of a second, it gives you the facility to discover split second timings for sports events, including lap times; for movie making, tape recording, etc. And however you use it, event timing remains unaffected.

Because when you stop the watch, it continues to record time. So you can record winner's time and, a split second later, runner-up time too. All the while the seconds flicker just as they do on a TV screen at major sports events. And it will store time totals as long as you need them.

You can even refer back to time and date without affecting stopwatch timing.

Alarm.
With a watch as accurate as this, time-wasting is eliminated. Apart from waking you, the alarm can be set to remind you of appointments, broadcast programmes you specially want to catch, when to leave for the train. It can even be set to chime every hour of the day.

Night Reading.
You won't have to grope for a box of matches or the nearest lamp-post when it's dark.
For night reading you simply press the button again and a light illuminates the digits.

Battery Indicator.
A flashing readout reminds you when it's time to change the battery (usually about once a year).
And, unlike most quartz watches, you can even change it yourself. Instead of paying a dealer to do it for you.

Elegance.
Certainly this Buler chronograph alarm analogue watch out-performs many of its competitors. But to really appreciate it you have to see it, have to feel it on your wrist. Only then can you recognise its true quality.

Cheaper chronographs don't feel or look as good, and neither are they analogue. Certainly they don't have that mark of quality that comes only from the Swiss watchmaker's hand.

Fully guaranteed.
Your Buler Swiss chronograph and analogue watch is covered by the maker's full one-year guarantee. And comes complete with full instructions.

To order, simply complete the coupon below and post it off today. Within 21–28 days your chronograph and analogue watch will arrive.

If you're not completely satisfied with it, just return it within 30 days and we'll refund your money.

Scotcade Ltd
33-34 HIGH STREET BRIDGNORTH SHROPSHIRE WV16 4HG

To Scotcade Ltd, 33–34 High Street, Bridgnorth, Shropshire WV16 4HG.

Please send me _____ Analogue chronograph(s) (AQ--) at £91.90 each (inc £1.95 post, packing and insurance).

I enclose my cheque/postal order for £ _____

or please debit my Access card, No. _____

SIGNATURE _____

NAME _____

ADDRESS _____ (Block letters please)

_____

AC/01/02

Scotcade Ltd., Registered Office, 14 Grosvenor Place, London SW1. Registered No. 1148225 England. Allow 21–28 days for delivery. Delivery U.K. exc. Channel Islands.

© Scotcade Ltd. 1979

Take it in turns with the others in your group to talk about the product you have seen advertised.

5

(You are student D.) Begin by advising your partners how to solve *their* problems. Then tell them your problem:

You are a student and you think you are being held back in your class. The other students are always asking elementary questions and are much less fluent than you. Of course, you still make mistakes but you want to improve. Unfortunately you are in the top class in the school.

Ask your partners for advice.

When your problem has been discussed, look at activity 64.

6

You are all customers, and the students in the other group are shopkeepers. Go from shop to shop and complain *politely* about the following:

1 Quartz watch (£39.95) – loses one minute a day.
2 Dry-cleaned trousers (£1.00) – dirtier than before.
3 Book (£4.95) – two pages near the middle are blank.
4 Two oranges (15p each) – rotten in the middle.
5 Bottle of wine (£2.40) – funny taste.
6 Record (£5.99) – a lot of surface noise.
7 Briefcase (£23.50) – handle has come loose.
8 Cassette tape (£1.50) – broke the first time you used it.

When all your complaints have been dealt with satisfactorily, look at activity 27.

7

(You are student C.)

1 Listen to A's opinion on a topic and say what you think about it. Then listen to B's opinion on another topic and say what you think about that.

2 Persuade your partners to agree with your opinion that:
HOUSEHOLD PETS ARE DISGUSTING – people should not be allowed to keep cats and dogs in their houses, they spread diseases...

3 Listen to A's views on another topic and say what you think. Then listen to B's views on another topic and say what you think.

4 Persuade your partners to agree with your opinion that:
ADVERTISING IS GREAT FUN – magazines and TV programmes are improved by witty, colourful advertisements, life is made more interesting...

When you have finished, discuss what you did with the rest of the class.

8 You are an expert on William Shakespeare, the man on the £20 note. Study the outline of his life below for a few minutes.

**WILLIAM SHAKESPEARE
1564 – 1616**

Born at Stratford-upon-Avon, son of prosperous tradesman. Educated at Stratford Grammar School.
Married Anne Hathaway 1582. Joined company of actors in 1589 at Globe Theatre in London. 1593 Earl of Southampton became his patron.

Probably wrote 36 plays – 18 published during his lifetime. Also sonnets and other poems.

Wrote popular comedies, such as: *Twelfth Night, Much Ado About Nothing, A Midsummer Night's Dream, Taming of the Shrew, As You Like It.*

Wrote many historical plays, such as: *Henry IV Parts 1 and 2, Henry V, Richard III.*

Best loved still today for great tragedies: *Romeo and Juliet, Hamlet, Othello, Macbeth, King Lear, Antony and Cleopatra.*

Died 1616, age 52. Buried Stratford Churchyard.
1623 first folio edition of 36 plays published.

*Shakespeare's vocabulary was 20,000 words.
Many of his turns of phrase have become part of the English language:*
   'in my mind's eye' (Hamlet)
   'every dog will have his day' (Hamlet)

The idea is to find out as much as possible about the four famous people on the banknotes by asking each other questions. Take it in turns to be asked questions.

When you have finished, discuss what you did with the rest of the class.

---

9 If you were cut off at home by snow-drifts tonight, how would this affect your short-term plans? What would you not be able to do then?

Discuss this possibility thoroughly. Then look at activity 58.

---

10 Here is another subject you feel strongly about:
MACHINES SHOULD DO ROUTINE JOBS

Again you have three minutes to prepare your arguments. You believe that it is an insult to ask people to do boring routine jobs (like cleaning or typing) and that machines should do this sort of work.
Try to make your partners listen to your arguments.

When you have finished, discuss what you did with the rest of the class.

11 Your partner is going to play three different roles – boss, friend and teacher – while you ask for permission in an appropriate way. Make these requests *in this order* and if necessary explain why you want to do them:

1 Ask your boss to let you change your holiday from next week to the week after.
2 Ask your friend if you can borrow his or her dictionary.
3 Ask your teacher to let you go and make a phone call now.
4 Ask your boss again. This time you want to take the Friday off before your holiday begins. Say why this is necessary.
5 Ask your friend again. This time you want to keep the dictionary over the weekend. Say why.
6 Ask your teacher to let you go to the bank immediately. Say why it is so urgent.
7 Now, ask your boss to let you change your holiday *back* to next week now. Say why.
8 Now, ask your friend to let you borrow his or her grammar book as well as the dictionary over the weekend. Say why.
9 Now, ask your teacher to let you go to the bank *again*. Say why.

When you have finished, go to activity 84.

---

12 Your new shoes got wet in a shower of rain and were permanently stained. When you took them back to the shop, they refused to accept responsibility and told you it was your own fault.
Tell your friend how angry you are.

Look at activity 145, next.

---

13 Your two friends have agreed to spend the weekend with you. Here are your ideas on what to do:

SATURDAY Spend day on the beach – enjoying sun and relaxing.
Take picnic lunch (tell them what food you'll take).
Evening: party at Michael's (tell them about Michael's last party which was really great).
SUNDAY Meet rest of class at railway station.
All go to London for the day (tell the others what you can see and do there).
Stay till late – go to a restaurant run by people from your country (tell the others what they can eat there).

Take it in turns to present your plans to each other. Be enthusiastic!
Then decide which plan sounds best. If necessary, work out a compromise plan.

14
1 Your friend has just come back after borrowing your new car and seems a bit nervous...
2 Your friend asked you to paint his or her lounge. Unfortunately, while you were painting, the tin of paint fell over and went all over the floor. Break it gently because the new carpet has been ruined.

When you have finished, look at activity 95.

15 Find out why your friend looks depressed.

When you have cheered your friend up, discuss what you did with the rest of the class. That's the end of the activity.

---

16 (You are still in group B.) This time it's your turn to take the initiative and start conversations with people in group A. The idea of this activity is to give you a chance to *experiment* and build up your confidence – in real life you need to be quite brave to start conversations.

End each conversation by saying: 'Well, I've really enjoyed talking to you, but I must be off now. See you later, perhaps.' Then find another member of group A to start a conversation with. Stand up and find someone to talk to now!

After a number of conversations, your teacher will tell you to stop. Then there will be time to discuss what you did with the rest of the class.

---

17 You are staying at a hotel. It is 6 o'clock in the morning and the guest in the next room has just woken you up. He or she is only wearing a towel. Find out what he or she wants and agree or refuse to do the things you are asked. As it's early in the morning you're *not* feeling very helpful or bright.

When you have finished, discuss what you did with the rest of the class. Then student B should look at activity 69 and student C at activity 100.

---

18 Your friend is late and in a bad temper. Find out why and try to calm him or her down.

Look at activity 12, next.

19 You are very happy to be able to help your friend, A, with his or her new flat. Begin by making a list of the things *you want* to do to help. You aren't worried about how hard you have to work and are free all day and evening.

Wait for A to welcome you to the flat before you begin to decide together what needs doing and who is going to do what.

---

20 This is a subject you feel *very* strongly about:
NO INTERFERENCE IN PERSONAL LIBERTY (for example, the attempt to make smoking illegal in public places)

You have three minutes to think and make notes of the reasons why you think that the individual should have freedom to choose where to smoke, how much to drink, how fast to drive and so on.
Try to convince your partners that you are right – make them listen to your reasons.

When you have finished, discuss and analyse your performance. Then look at activity 133.

---

21 You have several pieces of bad news for your friends. Break each piece of news gently and say how disappointed you are. When your friends tell you their bad news, be sympathetic.

1 You passed the exam, but your friends didn't. You got a Distinction.
2 Your friends both left the play after the first act because it was boring. You stayed on and the second and third acts were fantastic.
3 You've spilt your friends' drinks on the floor.
4 Your car has a puncture, so you can't get to the party in time.
5 You wanted to go to London and thought your friends were both busy – you went alone and had a miserable time.
6 You now have to discuss this activity with the rest of the class. Tell your friends.

---

22 Your only pleasure in life is your TV. When you can't sleep, you love watching the late film. You are *slightly* deaf.

When your neighbour knocks, pretend not to hear at first. Then try to satisfy his or her complaint. After that, look at activity 48.

23 Look at this diary page. It shows what happened to *you* last Friday:

Friday 13 March

First day back at work after holiday. Bad start – missed train. Had to take car, parking very difficult in town. 30 minutes late.

Piles of work – letters to reply to, reports to read, visits to arrange. Jane away ill, so no help. Ted popped in for a chat, happened to mention that Mr Green is leaving. Asked about his job – apparently it was advertised while I was on holiday. Not fair! Closing date last week! Rang Mr Brown to find out more – he said no chance.

Lunch in pub. Ted suggested phoning Chairman's secretary about job. Good idea!

Phoned her. She said interviews were today – many external applicants. Short list of 6 already made. Further interviews this afternoon. Can I be added to this list? Probably not but phone Chairman.

Waited ages to get through (he was very busy). In the end managed to speak to him. Persuaded him that internal candidate should be preferred to outsiders. Got the job!

Evening: celebration. Drove home but on the way some idiot in green car leaving pub car park hit my car – hooted loudly to warn him. Only minor damage to his car – didn't stop to argue. But when I got home I found my car was quite badly damaged. Garage estimate £150! Felt very upset.

Begin by asking your partner exactly what happened to him or her last Friday. When you have found out everything, your partner will try to find out what happened to you. Don't remember too easily – wait to be asked specific questions.

When you have finished, discuss what you did with the rest of the class.

24 You have a toothache. And a headache. It's Sunday. And it's pouring with rain. And your girlfriend (or boyfriend) has left you. You had an argument and she's gone abroad and you can't contact her to make it up. Tell your friend about it all.

When you feel better, look at activity 139.

---

25 This time it's your turn to go round meeting different students and asking them to do things. Ask your partner to do the first thing in the list below, and when he or she has agreed, move on to talk to another student A. Treat everyone you meet as a friend, but not as a very close friend. Stand up first.

1 You need a good street map of the town, but you haven't got time to go to the bookshop.
2 You feel like some chocolate, but can't be bothered to go and buy it yourself.
3 Your airline flight departure needs to be confirmed, but you can't go to the travel agent's yourself.
4 You want to go to the cinema, but don't know when the performances start. Get someone else to ring up for you.
5 You are feeling ill and can't go to school. Get someone to telephone the school and tell them.
6 You are going to Scotland for the weekend. Get someone to call your landlady and tell her.
7 You are busy and can't talk to this friend for two or three minutes. Ask him or her to wait.
8 You have some homework to finish. You can't talk to this friend for fifteen minutes. Ask him or her to come back later.
9 You're on your way to a lecture. You can't talk until it's finished. Ask your friend to wait until then.
10 Ask your partner to go back to his or her own seat and be ready to discuss this activity with the rest of the class.

Go back to your own seat.

---

26 Now it's your turn to play the part of the accident-prone student. Your hostess has been out for the evening and when she gets back you have some bad news for her:

She left your meal in the oven, but you forgot about it and it got burnt. That's why there's the smell of smoke all over the house.
You helped yourself to a glass of wine to calm yourself down and spilt a whole glass on her new white carpet. It was the cat's fault – it jumped on your lap and knocked the glass out of your hand.
The telephone rang several times but you never got to it in time to answer it.
You didn't remember to pick up her little son, Billy, from Mrs Green's till 11 o'clock. Mrs Green was angry and said she wouldn't look after him ever again.

When you have finished, discuss what you did with the rest of the class.

27 Now it's your turn to be shopkeepers. Each of you should sit down in a separate place (pretending to be in a shop), and wait for a customer to come in. Be polite to each customer and try to be as helpful as possible.

When there seem to be no more customers, you can shut up shop for the day and discuss your performance with the rest of the class.

---

28 You have just got the sack. You arrived late and were unintentionally rude to your boss. It was a good job. There's no chance of getting such a good job in another company. Tell your friend.

When you feel better, look at activity 68.

---

29 You have cut this advertisement out of a newspaper. The product advertised seems really good – fantastic value in fact. Persuade your partners to spend their money on this:

The new Micro Quartz Alarm Clock.
Incredible accuracy wherever you want it. £7.95.
(+p&p)

Accurate to within 180 seconds a year, this miniscule battery-powered quartz alarm clock gives you precision wherever you go.

Measuring only 2⅜"x 2⅜"x 1³⁄₁₆", light yet robust, here's a clock that combines the famous accuracy of Quartz timekeeping with elegantly compact dimensions and portability.

Three years ago, we introduced our first Micro clock at only £10.95. The response was overwhelming.

Now, despite crippling inflation, this new model is being offered at an incredible £7.95.
(+£1.45 p&p).

99.999% accurate.
Originally devised for scientists, who require accuracy of the highest order, the basic principle of Quartz timekeeping is simple.

When the current is applied to the pure Quartz crystal, the atoms vibrate at a constant speed of 4.194304 million times per second.

Miniaturised circuits translate this constant motion to indicate the time.

The Quartz clock uses this system to provide an unbeatable degree of accuracy. It will lose no more than 180 seconds per year. 99.999% accuracy.

Using a time standard – GPO or BBC pips – the clock can be set to the exact time (even the second hand is adjustable) which will then be maintained within the parameters stated.

Superb design.
Every aspect of this clock has been carefully thought out. The components were made by a Japanese company to ensure precision and quality.

The housing is of tough black ABS. An easily-available 1.5 volt alkaline battery will provide power for about a year.

The electronic alarm has been designed with a pleasant but insistent tone to wake you without annoying you. And the alarm cut-off is logically positioned on the side; a simple slider that means you don't have to fumble sleepily to turn it off.

This clock will be perfect anywhere in your home or office. And it comes complete with a leatherette carrying pouch which makes it ideal for travelling.

To order your clock, simply fill in the coupon. In 21 to 28 days it'll arrive at your door with a full year's guarantee.

☎ **CREDIT CARD HOLDERS MAY TELEPHONE 07462 5744 AND PLACE ORDER IMMEDIATELY WITHOUT COMPLETING THE COUPON.**

And if you're not happy with your clock, simply return it to us within 30 days and we'll refund your money.

Scotcade Ltd.
33-34 High Street, Bridgnorth, Shropshire WV16 4HG.

Previous version £10.95. Save £3.

To: Scotcade Ltd, 33-34 High Street, Bridgnorth, Shropshire WV16 4HG.
Please send me ____ Micro Quartz clock(s), (MP--) at £9.40 (inc. £1.45 p&p and insurance) each. Battery not included. I enclose cheque/postal order for £ _____ or debit my Access account.

No. ____
Signature ____
Name ____ BLOCK LETTERS PLEASE.
Address ____
____
AC/01/06

Scotcade Ltd, Registered Office, 14 Grosvenor Place, London SW1. Registered No. 1148225 England. Allow 21 to 28 days for delivery. Delivery is subject to availability. UK exc. Channel Islands.

CALLERS MAY BUY FROM OUR SHOP IN **BIRMINGHAM** PARADISE STREET. **BRIGHTON** CHURCHILL SQUARE. **BRISTOL** 17 BROAD WIER. **CROYDON** 1135 WHITGIFT CENTRE. **EDINBURGH** 43 SOUTH BRIDGE. **GLASGOW** ANDERSTON CROSS CENTRE. **LEEDS** OPPOSITE CORN EXCHANGE. **LEICESTER** 7 SIDDONS WALK, HAYMARKET CENTRE. **LIVERPOOL** 33 LIME STREET. **LONDON EC1** 19 HOLBORN VIADUCT. **LONDON EC3** 5 CAMOMILE STREET (OFF BISHOPSGATE). **LONDON NW4** BRENT CROSS SHOPPING CENTRE. **LONDON SW18** ARNDALE CENTRE. **MANCHESTER** 5 SHAMBLES SQUARE. **NEWCASTLE** 24 NEWGATE CENTRE. **NORTHAMPTON** 10 THE FRIARY GROSVENOR CENTRE. **NOTTINGHAM** 71 MAID MARIAN WAY. **READING** 20 MARKET PLACE. **SHEFFIELD** 12 ARUNDEL GATE. **SOUTHAMPTON** 59 EAST STREET CENTRE.

Take it in turns with the others in your group to talk about the product you have seen advertised.

30

(You are student B.)

1 Listen to A's opinion on a topic and say what you think about it.

2 Persuade your partners to agree with your opinion that:
BOARDING SCHOOLS ARE EXCELLENT – children learn more if they're separated from their parents, they also learn to socialize better...

3 Listen to C's opinion on another topic. Say what you think. Then listen to A's opinion on another topic and say what you think.

4 Persuade your partners to agree with your opinion that:
SOFT DRUGS LIKE MARIJUANA SHOULD BE LEGALIZED – Cigarettes are more harmful to the health, marijuana is not illegal in many parts of the world...

5 Listen and react to C's opinion on another topic.

When you have finished, discuss what you did with the rest of the class.

31

Your group is planning a voyage by car from Algiers to Cape Town. You need to be as well-equipped as possible without spending too much money.
Decide what equipment, clothes etc. you are going to take and tell the rest of the class. If you disagree about an item, report it as a possible or probable item for inclusion. Give reasons why you need or don't need each item.
You are definitely going on this voyage, by the way – so don't spend any time deciding if it's a good idea to go or not!

✓ = Yes, definitely
✓? = Yes, probably
?? = Perhaps
✗? = No, probably not
✗ = No, definitely not

32

1 Your friend lent you his or her car this morning and while parking you put a scratch all along the side. Break it gently because the car was new last month and you promised to be very, very careful.

2 Your friend has been painting your lounge while you were out – you hope he or she has made a good job of it...

When you have finished, look at activity 134.

33

(You are student B.) Begin by advising A how to solve his or her problem. Then tell your partners your own problem:

You are a student away from home and you are finding life very depressing. You don't think your English is improving and you are homesick. Your course lasts another six months.

Ask your partners for advice.

When your problem has been discussed, advise C and D how to solve their problems.

When all these problems have been discussed, look at activity 126.

34 Your neighbour keeps on parking his or her car in front of your house, partially blocking your garage entrance. This makes it difficult for you to get your car in and out. Knock on your neighbour's door and complain.

When you are satisfied, look at activity 22.

---

35 (You are in group A.) Make sure each member of the group has time to say what he or she thinks. Your committee has been asked to prepare a report on:
YOUR MAIN DIFFICULTIES WITH ENGLISH VOCABULARY

Your discussion should include: the difficulty of remembering new words, how to decide if a new word is one you need to learn to *use* or simply just recognize, learning to use words appropriately, different individual students needing to know different vocabulary etc.

When you are ready, report your findings to the rest of the class and ask them for their comments on your report. Then listen to group B's report and group C's report and comment on them.

36
1 Say hallo to your friend and find out if he or she is well.
2 Ask your friend to pay you back the £10 he or she owes you. You need it to pay your exam enrolment fee *today*.
3 You promised your friend that you would telephone the theatre to book some tickets last week but it slipped your mind. Now there are no seats left. Break it gently because your friend was really looking forward to seeing the play.

When you have finished, look at activity 14.

---

37 You feel fine today. It's a sunny day and you're enjoying yourself. Your friend doesn't seem so cheerful, though. Find out what the matter is and be sympathetic.

When you have cheered your friend up, look at activity 24.

---

38 (You are in group B.) In this activity a number of people from group A are going to start conversations with you. There's no need to be unfriendly, of course, but let them do all the work. Let them start each conversation and find a way of finishing it. Let them ask the questions. Stand up for this activity.

After a number of conversations, your teacher will give you a signal to look at activity 16.

39 Here is another subject you feel strongly about:
AUTOMATION MEANS UNEMPLOYMENT

Again you have three minutes to prepare your arguments. You believe that more machines means less work for humans and that this will bring more unemployment. Try to make your partners listen to your arguments.

When you have finished, discuss what you did with the rest of the class.

---

40 You are an expert on the *early* career of the Beatles. Your partner will ask you questions to find out what you know about it. Treat your partner as an acquaintance, not a close friend.

```
THE BEATLES 1956 - 1964

Richard Starkey (Ringo Starr) born 7.7.40
John Winston Lennon            born 9.10.40, died 8.12.80
Paul McCartney                 born 18.6.42
George Harrison                born 25.2.43

1956-58  Their early groups were called: the Quarrymen, Wump and the Werbles,
         the Rainbows, John and the Moondogs.
1959     John, Paul, George and two others became the Beatles.
1960     They played at the Cavern Club in Liverpool and in Hamburg.
1961     Brian Epstein (manager of a record shop) became their manager.  He made
         them wear suits and cut their hair.
1962     Beatles signed up by George Martin of Parlophone Records. He became the
         producer of all their recordings.  Ringo Starr joined the group,
         replacing the two others who had left.  Love Me Do released - went to
         number 17 in the charts.
1963     Five number 1 records: Please Please Me, From Me to You, Twist and Shout,
         She Loves You, I Want to Hold Your Hand.  First tours of Britain.  Start
         of 'Beatlemania'.  Crowds went mad.

         Sunday Times: '... greatest composers since Beethoven.'
         Prime Minister: '... our best exports.'

1964     Success in USA.  Tours of North America, Europe, Australia.  First film
         A Hard Day's Night directed by Richard Lester.
```

When your partner is satisfied with the answers you have given, look at activity 57.

41   In this part of the activity you are *yourself*. The idea is to go round the class meeting the students with badges or labels who are playing roles and speak to them appropriately.
The list below shows the things which need to be done – you must make the requests in the order below. Remember that your language must be polite enough to be effective, but not so polite as to sound sarcastic!

1 You want a cigarette. You have left yours at home.
2 You want to know what stamp to put on a postcard to a British address.
3 You have lost your gloves. You want someone to help you find them.
4 You have to leave the room. You want someone to keep an eye on your things.
5 You have bought some new batteries for your radio. You want someone to put them in for you.
6 You don't understand the word 'role'.
7 Your arms are full and you want to turn off the light.
8 Tell someone you have a headache. See if they can help you.
9 Ask your partner to go back to his or her seat and look at activity 85, while you sit down and look at activity 123.

---

42   Your friend seems very cross this morning. Find out what's the matter and try to calm him or her down.

Look at activity 130, next.

---

43   (You are student A.) You begin by telling your partners *your* problem:

You are a student and you are not happy in your class. Although your English is as good as theirs, your class-mates often laugh at you when you speak. You have spoken to your teacher about this, but he or she says this is the best class for you.

Ask your partners for advice.

When your problem has been discussed, find out B's problem and advise him or her what to do. Then C's and D's problems.

When all these problems have been discussed, look at activity 144.

44 You are an expert on Florence Nightingale, the woman on the £10 note. Study the outline of her life below for a few minutes.

FLORENCE NIGHTINGALE
1820 – 1910

Born in Florence, Italy, of wealthy parents.

In 1854 she took a staff of nurses to Scutari, Turkey, to care for wounded soldiers from Crimean War (England and France v. Russia). Reduced death rate from 42% to 2%.

Before then nurses were regarded as little better than prostitutes. Regarded as the founder of the nursing profession.

She walked through the wards with a lamp, comforting the patients. She became known as the Lady with the Lamp.

Lived in retirement, but worked continuously to improve the training of nurses. Died 1910, age 90.

A Nightingale is a song-bird which winters in Africa and breeds in Europe. Its song is the most beautiful of bird songs and is best heard at night, when other birds are silent.

The idea is to find out as much as you can about the famous people on the banknotes by asking each other questions. Take it in turns to be asked questions.

When you have finished, discuss what you did with the rest of the class.

---

45 Well, it's time for us to say goodbye. Thank you for working through these communication activities. We hope you've found them useful and enjoyable.

Goodbye, and good luck with using what you've learnt from *Functions of English*!

46 Look at this report of a simple conversation. Work *alone* and write down in dialogue form the actual words that were spoken. Begin like this:

Aunt Mary: Oh dear. It's eight o'clock already. It's time I began getting ready to go...

Aunt Mary gave an exclamation of surprise when she saw it was already eight o'clock, and said it was time she thought about leaving. She asked John whether he would mind calling a taxi for her, explaining that her train left at nine, and she didn't want to miss it. John reassured his aunt and said that he would drive her to the station – the car was outside the door and it would only take ten minutes. Aunt Mary hesitated at first, but John managed to persuade her that he had nothing else to do that evening, and that it would be no trouble at all. She eventually agreed, so John offered her another cup of coffee, which she gratefully accepted.

When you have finished, give your written dialogue to your partner. Ask your partner to write a report giving only the main points of the conversation (without looking at this page, of course). Your partner will ask you to do the same with his or her dialogue.

When you have both finished, compare your report with the report your partner started with in activity 111. Discuss the differences.

---

47 (You are student B.) Your partner is going to ask you to do something. If the request is polite enough to persuade you to do it, agree. You may want to know *why* he or she wants you to do it.

After the first conversation *stand up* and another student will ask you something else. Stand up during these conversations but do not walk around. Each of the people that ask you things are people you have met before, but they are not close friends.

Another student will tell you what to do when you have finished.

---

48 Your friend never buys his or her own drinks, and always waits until you or someone else offers one. Your friend has enough money. (It's the same with cigarettes.)

The time has come to complain politely.

When your conversation is finished, look at activity 112.

---

49 You're in a good mood today, but your friend looks unhappy. Try to be sympathetic.

When your friend feels better, look at activity 28.

50

This is a subject you feel *very* strongly about:
NO SMOKING IN PUBLIC PLACES

You have three minutes to think and make notes of the reasons why you think it should be *illegal* to smoke in trains, restaurants, planes, cinemas, bars, theatres and other public places.

Try to convince your partners that you are right – make them listen to your reasons.

When you have finished, discuss and analyse your performance. Then look at activity 98.

51

(You are in group A.) In pairs, work out a set of instructions for each of these activities:
1 How to play your favourite indoor game.
2 How to make a good cup of coffee.

When you are ready, get together with a pair from group B. Explain to them carefully how to do one of the two activities you are an expert on.
Then listen to one of their activities and ask questions. Then back to your second activity before they take their second turn.

52

You are an expert on making tea. Study these instructions before explaining to your partner exactly how to make a nice cup of tea. Do not look at the instructions below while you are explaining.

How to make a NICE CUPPA....

Heat Water in a kettle!	Warm Teapot... empty hot water	Tea: one spoonful per person.... + one for the pot!
Add boiling water (Take the pot to the kettle).	Allow to brew for about 3 mins.	Cold milk and sugar to taste. HAVE A NICE PIECE OF CAKE WITH IT!

When you have finished, your partner will explain to you how to do something else. Ask questions and get a detailed explanation. Imagine you have no idea about the subject. Repeat the instructions back to your partner to show you have fully understood.

53

(You are student A.) In this part of the activity, you get up and go from one sitting person (student B) to the next. You are trying to find someone to help you with your problems. But this time it may not be so easy to get people to agree because they are all strangers. Remember that you must speak appropriately and this depends on *who* you ask and *what* you want them to do.

When you have found someone to help you with the first problem, move on to the second problem in the list.

1 You need a pen.
2 You don't know the way to the station.
3 Your watch has stopped.
4 You don't understand the word 'appropriate'.
5 Your suitcase is very heavy, you can't lift it by yourself.
6. It's very cold with the window open and you aren't tall enough to reach it yourself.
7 You're in a shop looking for a present for your mother. You can't decide what to buy, so you would like some advice.
8 You're dying for a cigarette.
9 Ask your partner to look at activity 108, while you look at activity 150.

54

You have two young children – they cry all night and keep you awake.
Your neighbour is about to knock at your door.

Try to satisfy your neighbour's complaint and then look at activity 65.

55

Try to interest your friend in these plans:

Going to the cinema this evening.
Helping you with some home-decorating.
Spending some time studying together.
Going to a football match on Saturday.
Having a good lunch together tomorrow.

When you have succeeded in arousing his or her interest, look at activity 122. Tell your friend to look at activity 147.

56

Your partner is going to ask you for permission to do certain things. In each conversation you switch from one role to another. Your partner will make the requests in this order, so follow these instructions.

1 You are the boss. Your partner is one of your most reliable workers.
2 You are a friend. You are on good terms.
3 You are the teacher. Your partner is a student who often misses lessons.
4 You are the boss again. Ask your employee why he or she didn't say this before.
5 You are a friend. You have to write an essay over the weekend.
6 You are the teacher again. This lesson is a very important one.
7 You are the boss again. You are getting tired of your employee's changing his or her mind.
8 You are a friend. Your class has a grammar test on Monday.
9 You are the teacher. You want everyone in the class to be present during this very important lesson.

When you have finished, go to activity 114.

57

This time you want information about the later career of the Beatles from your partner. Find the facts missing from the information sheet below by asking appropriate questions. Treat your partner as an acquaintance, not as a close friend.

```
THE BEATLES 1965 - 1970

1965 Tour of USA - $....... from Shea Stadium concert in ......... . ............
     ...... was their 10th British number 1.  Second film ..... in colour
     directed by .............. .
1966 World tour, including ..... . John Lennon: '............................
     ....................' Last live concert, .............. . ........
     released.
1967 Sergeant Pepper's Lonely Hearts Club Band praised by ....... and ..... .
     All You Need is Love seen on TV by ... million viewers. ............
     committed suicide.  TV film Magical Mystery Tour described by critics as
     '..................'.
1968 Studying in India with ............. . The Beatles 'White Album'
     ............ many fans.  Excellent ....... film ................
     based on Beatles songs, directed by George Dunning.
1969 Disagreement between .... and ..... John married ........, Paul married
     ............ . .......... recorded.
1970 Premiere of film ........ - no Beatles attended.  Paul: '... I didn't leave
     the Beatles, the Beatles have left the Beatles - but .....................
     ..............................' The four Beatles .......................... .
```

When you are satisfied with the answers you have received, discuss what you found out with the rest of the class.

58 If you became so rich you never had to work again, how would this affect your long-term ambitions?

Discuss this possibility thoroughly. Then discuss the whole of the activity with the rest of the class.

---

59 It's been one of those days – tell your friend about these events which have made you feel really depressed:

You've lost your wallet.
You've got to buy your sister a present.
You feel sick after overeating last night.
You missed the bus to work this morning.
You got very wet in the rain because you had to walk.
You've got an exam tomorrow and you're going to fail.
You have just had a row with your girlfriend (or boyfriend).
You are very tired.

When you feel happier, look at activity 66.

---

60 You are all shopkeepers. Each of you should sit down in a separate place (pretending to be in a shop), and wait for a customer to come in. Be polite to each customer and try to be as helpful as possible.

When there seem to be no more customers today, you can close your shop for lunch and look at activity 90.

---

61 (You are student B.) During this part of the activity you will be playing a role. Get together with the other student Bs and decide who will play which of the roles below. If possible, make sure everyone has a different role. Then make a badge or label to identify yourself.

I am your   BOSS
I am your   ASSISTANT
I am a   STRANGER your own age
I am your   LANDLADY
I am an   ELDERLY STRANGER
I am a   CHILD you know
I am the   HOTEL RECEPTIONIST
I am your   HEADMASTER

Now stand up. Different people will come up to you and make various requests. If they are polite enough and their requests are reasonable, agree to do what they ask. You can ask *why*.

Another student will tell you what to do at the end.

62 You have several pieces of bad news for your friends. Break each piece of news gently and say how disappointed you are. When your friends tell you their bad news, be sympathetic.

1. The film you all wanted to see isn't on this week.
2. Your friends didn't get the job, but you did.
3. You've been to the doctor. He says you and everyone you've been in contact with must stay in quarantine for a week. You spent last night with your friends.
4. None of you are allowed out (because you are ill). Your TV is broken and your hi-fi music centre is being repaired.
5. You tried phoning your friends to invite them to go to London with you, but you couldn't get through. So you went and had a miserable time.

---

63 First listen to your partner's problems and offer to help him or her with each of them. Then tell your partner your own problems and see if he or she offers to help you:

1. You have a terrible headache.
2. You have to phone your boss to say you're ill, but you're afraid to do it yourself.
3. You're dying for a cigarette.
4. Your watch has stopped.
5. A button has come off your shirt (or blouse) and has to be sewn back on.
6. You feel like a cup of tea.
7. You've written a letter which needs typing.
8. You're very nervous about a date you have this evening.

When you have finished, discuss what you did with the rest of the class.

---

64 Begin by helping your partners to solve their problems.
Then play this role yourself:

You are an 18-year-old girl and your boyfriend wants to move to the Shetland Isles. He can get a very good job there and he enjoys bird-watching and fishing. He wants you to go with him, but you aren't sure if it's a good idea. You know that the climate is very cold and that there is not much social life there. Your parents say you're too young to move so far away. What should you do?

When your partners have finished giving you advice, discuss what you did with the rest of the class.

---

65 Your neighbour's dog barks at you whenever you walk into your garden. Yesterday it chased you down the street, but luckily you escaped. When you complained to your neighbour's son he laughed at you.
Knock at your neighbour's door and complain.

When you are satisfied, look at activity 116.

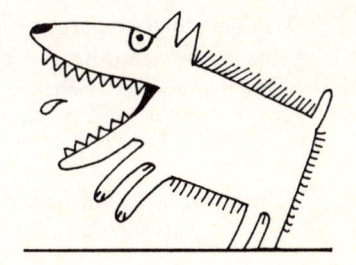

66 This time it's your friend who's depressed. Ask what's wrong and listen sympathetically. Try to cheer your friend up. Perhaps offer some advice or suggest something to take your friend's mind off his or her problems.

When your friend seems happier, discuss what you did with the rest of the class.

---

67 1 You borrowed £10 from your friend last week, promising to pay it back today. You haven't got the money. Break it gently.
2 Remind your friend about the theatre tickets he or she promised to book.

When you have finished, look at activity 32.

---

68 It's Sunday, your favourite day. It's raining but there are some good programmes on TV. Your friend doesn't look too happy, find out what the problem is.

When you have cheered your friend up, look at activity 78.

---

69 You are a business man or woman. You have a very busy day ahead with a meeting this afternoon and you have no time to do these trivial jobs yourself:

Order stationery: paper clips, drawing pins, typing paper
Buy the *Financial Times* and the *Economist*
Get birthday card, flowers, present for wife or husband
Put off Mr Robert's appointment to tomorrow
Type minutes of meeting (this will mean working late this evening)
Phone chairman to say when you will arrive to see him

Ask your assistant to do these jobs for you.

When you have finished, discuss what you did with the rest of the class and then look at activity 2.

---

70 (You are student A – you begin.)
1 Persuade your partners to agree with your opinion that:
WOMEN'S LIBERATION IS RIDICULOUS – women should stay at home, look after children ...

2 Listen to B's opinion about another topic and say what you think about it. Then listen to C's opinion about another topic.

3 Persuade your partners to agree with your opinion that:
DEVELOPING NUCLEAR POWER IS ESSENTIAL – oil and gas supplies are running out, nuclear energy is cheap, clean and plentiful ...

4 Listen to B's views and C's views on two more topics. Say what you think.

When you have finished, discuss what you did with the rest of the class.

71 You have just been cheated in a restaurant, which your friend recommended, called the Green Restaurant. The food was cold, the service was slow and you were over-charged by £2.
Tell your friend how angry you are.

When you have finished, discuss what you did with the rest of the class.

---

72 You have cut this advertisement out of a newspaper. The product advertised seems really good and amazing value. Persuade your partners to spend their money on the product:

SMALL ENOUGH TO CARRY, YET BIG ENOUGH TO SEE. THE CROWN PERSONAL TV. JUST £109.95.

SOMEHOW, portable televisions have never really managed to hit a happy medium. Either they're only portable if you happen to be built like Charles Atlas, or the screens are so small it's a waste of time watching them anyway.

But at the Scotcade price of £109.95 (+p&p), the Crown Personal TV is one that's actually got it right.

The screen is a respectable 4½", yet the Crown weighs just 7¾ lbs, excluding batteries.

And not only does it give you an extremely watchable television, it gives you AM and FM radio as well.

With a sound that's as clear as the picture.

The left hand dial covers all three television channels, the right hand one, radio.

And between the two is a special tuning eye for the radio which tells you when you're exactly on station.

In most areas you'll get superb reception from the telescopic antenna on top of the set, but if you have any trouble there's a socket for an external aerial.

There's also a socket for a personal earphone (provided), so you can watch or listen without disturbing anyone.

While you're in bed, or even while someone in the same room is listening to something else.

As with any true portable (and if you look around, you'll find that most "portables" aren't), the Crown gets its power from virtually anything that's handy.

It'll run on ordinary AC mains, a car battery (using a suitable lead), or eight easily available HP2 batteries clipped neatly into the back.

Which means that you can use it anywhere you can carry it.

In the kitchen, the garden, on a picnic, on a boat, in a caravan.

Anywhere.

To get your Crown Personal TV, all you have to do is fill in the coupon.

It'll arrive within 21 to 28 days, complete with a 12 month guarantee from the manufacturer.

And if you're not completely happy, simply return it within 30 days and we'll refund your money in full.

Scotcade Ltd.
33-34 High Street, Bridgnorth, Shropshire WV16 4HG.

To Scotcade Ltd., 33-34 High Street, Bridgnorth, Shropshire WV16 4HG
Please send me _____ Crown Portable Television(s) (PT–) at £112.90 (inc. £2.95 p&p).
I enclose cheque/postal order for
£_____ or debit my Diners Club/Access/ American Express/Barclaycard
No. _____
SIGNATURE _____
NAME _____
ADDRESS _____ (Block letters please)
CT 01/10
Scotcade Ltd., Registered Office, 14 Grosvenor Place, London SW1. Registered No. 1148225 Eng. Allow 21-28 days for delivery. Delivery U.K. exc. Channel Islands.
© Scotcade Ltd., 1978

Take it in turns with the others in your group to talk about the product you have seen advertised.

111

73   You are very happy to be able to help your friend, A, with his or her new flat. Begin by making a list of the things *you want* to do to help. You aren't worried about how hard you have to work and you are free all day and evening.

Wait for A to welcome you to the flat before you begin to decide together what needs doing and who is going to do what.

---

74   This is a subject you feel *very* strongly about:
SMOKING SHOULD BE ILLEGAL

You have three minutes to think and make notes of the reasons why you think that smoking is anti-social, unhealthy and destructive.
Try to convince your partners that you are right – make them listen to your reasons.

When you have finished, discuss and analyse your performance. Then look at activity 10.

---

75   (You are in group B.) Make sure each member of the group has time to say what he or she thinks. Your committee has been asked to prepare a report on:
YOUR MAIN DIFFICULTIES WITH ENGLISH GRAMMAR

Your discussion should include: particular areas of difficulty, your attitude to grammatical accuracy, problems of remembering, different individual students having different problems etc.

When you are ready, listen to group A's report and comment on their findings. Then give your report to the rest of the class and ask them for their comments on it. Then listen to and comment on group C's report.

---

76   Find out why your friend is cross. Try to calm him or her down. (The other day you recommended a restaurant to your friend, called the Green Parrot Restaurant.)

When you have finished, discuss what you did with the rest of the class.

---

77   Your two friends have agreed to spend the weekend with you. Here are your ideas on what to do:

SATURDAY   Get up late, have big breakfast.
Go to town: shopping (tell them what they can buy) and drink in a nice pub (tell them about the pub).
Evening: super meal in best restaurant in town (tell them about the last meal you had there).

SUNDAY   Morning: play golf (tell them about the course you're going to).
Lunch: in Chinese restaurant (tell them about the food you can eat there).
Afternoon: visit local castle (tell them about it).
Evening: watch TV (tell them about fantastic programme that's on).

Take it in turns to present your plans to each other. Be enthusiastic! Then decide which plan sounds best. If necessary, work out a compromise plan.

78 You have just heard that you have failed your exams. You had been offered a super job provided that you passed. You can't take them again. It means you've got no chance of getting a good job – probably you'll be out of work. Tell your friend.

When you feel better, look at activity 15.

---

79 Look at this diary page. It shows what happened to *you* last Friday:

> **Friday 13 March**
>
> Important day! Began badly: car wouldn't start, no taxis available, had to take bus. Late for interview. Also hot, sweaty, uncomfortable. Met other candidates – all cool, relaxed, confident.
>
> Interview seemed to go badly. Panel all aggressive – made me feel aggressive. Didn't make good impression. Asked to wait outside for result. Thought of going home then but decided to wait after all. Girl told me I was on the short list! Couldn't believe my ears. Second interview this afternoon.
>
> Afternoon interview went very well – they asked the right questions and I gave the right answers. They were just about to offer me a job (I thought) when phone call came for Chairman. Asked to wait outside. Called me back after quarter of an hour – told me vacancy now filled. Asked why. Internal applicants preferred to external ones! Protested but in vain.
>
> Evening: met friends at pub. They were very sympathetic – just leaving pub when big red estate car hit me. Maniac didn't stop – just drove off! No time to get the number. Damage £50. I was furious.

Begin by telling your partner what happened to you. Don't give too much information *unless* he or she asks a specific question. When your partner has found out enough, find out exactly what happened to him or her last Friday.

When you have finished, discuss what you did with the rest of the class.

80

(You are student A.) You want people to do various things for you. All the student Bs are people you know by name, but not close friends.

Ask your partner to do the first thing in the list below; when he or she has agreed, stand up and move on to talk to another student B. Then keep circulating round the class, moving from one person to the next. Ask each person you meet to do the *next* thing on the list.

1. You want a lemonade, but you have no change on you.
2. You want a pint of draught bitter, but you can't get to the bar.
3. You want a double whisky, but can't afford it.
4. You want a copy of the *Guardian*, but you haven't got time to go to the newsagent's and buy one.
5. You haven't got time to go to the bank yourself to get some money.
6. You want some theatre tickets, but you can't manage to get them yourself.
7. You want to sit down, but someone's books are on the seat.
8. You want to read, but someone is sitting in your light.
9. You want your friend to sit next to you, but someone else is sitting there.
10. Ask your original partner to look at activity 25, while you look at activity 110.

81

This time you are playing the part of your partner's assistant, he or she is your boss.

1. You have just got back from town. Your boss gave you £20 in small change to take to the bank but you put it down on the counter of a record shop while you were choosing a record and it disappeared. Break it gently because you were supposed to go only to the bank and come straight back.
2. You are annoyed because you have to work late for your boss this evening. You've cancelled a date and now it's too late to rearrange it.

When you have finished, report what happened to the rest of the class.

82

(You are in group B.) In pairs, work out a set of instructions for each of these activities:

1. How to cook one of your favourite dishes.
2. How to play your favourite outdoor sport.

When you are ready, get together with a pair from group A. Listen to their instructions on how to do one of their activities. Ask them questions as they go along.

Then it's your turn to instruct them how to do one of your two activities. Then they have their second turn before you explain your second activity.

83

(You are student C.) Begin by advising A and B how to solve *their* problems. Then tell your partners your own problem:

You are a student and you seem to be making no progress at all. You can't remember yesterday's lessons and you don't understand half of what your teacher says in class. Your teacher says you are in the right class for your level.

Ask your partners for advice.
When your problem has been discussed, advise D how to solve his or her problem. Then look at activity 106.

84 Your partner is now going to ask you for permission to do various things. In each conversation you switch from one role to another. Don't agree too easily to everything! Follow the instructions in this order.

1 You are a friend. It's a bit stuffy in this room.
2 You are the boss. You have a rule about personal phone calls on the office phone. Normally you turn a blind eye to short local calls, though.
3 You are your partner's landlady. You are planning to watch BBC2 this evening.
4 You are a friend. You are happy to have *one* window open.
5 You are the boss. You do not normally allow staff to make long-distance phone calls.
6 You are your partner's landlady. Your lounge is rather small and your sister is coming round this evening.
7 You are a friend. You have a cold and think you might have flu coming on.
8 You are the boss. You have just sent a memo round the office forbidding personal phone calls on the company's phones.
9 You are the landlady. Your husband has told you that he wants to watch the football match on ITV this evening.

When you have finished, discuss what you did with the rest of the class.

---

85 In this part of the activity you are *yourself* and it's your turn now to go round making requests. Make the requests in the order below and make sure you speak appropriately to the people playing different roles. Remember that you must be polite enough to be effective, but that if you are too polite you may sound sarcastic.

1 You want a light for your cigarette.
2 You want to send a letter to the USA but you don't know what stamp to put on the envelope.
3 You don't understand the word 'sarcastic'.
4 You want to fit a new light bulb but you need someone to hold the chair steady while you climb up.
5 You want a lift home because you haven't got any money for the bus or a taxi.
6 You want this person to speak more slowly, because you find it hard to understand him or her.
7 You can't open the door. It seems to be jammed. You need help.
8 You have dropped your pen behind a bookcase. See if someone will help you to get it.
9 Ask your partner to go back to his or her seat while you go back to yours.

Discuss what you did with the rest of the class.

---

86 You are an English housewife. You have a student lodging with you. You have just returned home after a nice evening out – the student seems nervous. Find out if he or she:

had a nice time while you were out.   got the bread for tomorrow's breakfast.
remembered to feed the cat.   knows why the front door lock seems stiff.

After your conversation, look at activity 26.

87 Begin by studying this strip cartoon. Decide how you can make your narration as interesting as possible. Add *detail* and *dialogue*. Imagine what had happened *before* the first scene and what happened *after* the last scene.

First listen to your partner's narration of a different story. Encourage your partner to give you plenty of detail by asking questions.

88 On your way here you had an accident on your bicycle. A motorist opened his door suddenly and knocked you off. Your bicycle was damaged and you hurt your foot. Instead of apologizing the motorist accused you of carelessness and drove off quickly. Tell your friend how angry you are.

Look at activity 76, next.

---

89 Your best friend had a party last Saturday and didn't invite you. You were upset because you heard about the party from an acquaintance the next day. (And your friend still hasn't paid you back the £5 he or she borrowed last month.)
Raise the matter tactfully with your friend.

When your conversation is finished, discuss this activity with the rest of the class.

---

90 Now it's your turn to be customers. Go from shop to shop and complain *politely* about the following:

1 Shirt (£10.00) – stain on the back of the collar.
2 Ball point pen (50p) – leaked all over your jacket.
3 Milk (18p) – sour.
4 Book (£2.95) – supposed to be new but pencil notes inside.
5 Shoes (£16.99) – heel came off.
6 Stereo headphones (£25.00) – buzzing in one ear.
7 Pullover (£4.00 in sale) – worn out at elbow after four weeks.
8 Alarm clock (£6.49) – not loud enough to wake you up.

When all your complaints have been dealt with satisfactorily, discuss your performance with the rest of the class.

---

91 Tell your partner about the following problems you have and see if he or she offers to help you with them. You can decide whether to accept the offer or refuse it politely:

1 You have a difficult essay to write, and you don't know how to approach it.
2 You meant to get a newspaper this morning and don't have enough time to get it now.
3 You feel like a cup of coffee.
4 You're short of money – £5 would be enough.
5 You can't get your car to start.
6 A button has just come off your coat, but you can't find it.
7 You've written a letter which needs posting.
8 You have a sore throat and can't stop coughing.

Now listen to your partner's problems and offer to help with each of them.

92 You are an expert on the Duke of Wellington, the man on the £5 note. Study the outline of his life below for a few minutes.

THE DUKE OF WELLINGTON
1769 – 1852

Born Arthur Wellesley in Ireland. Educated at Eton. Entered army in 1787. As major-general he achieved victories in India in 1803. Became *Sir* Arthur Wellesley.

Commanded English army in Peninsular War (England v. France). Drove the French out of Spain in 1814. Became first Duke of Wellington.

Defeated Napoleon at Waterloo, Belgium, 1815. Became most influential man in Europe.

Became Prime Minister 1828. Died in 1852, age 83. Buried in St Paul's Cathedral, London.

Wellingtons are a popular sort of rubber boot, worn by children, farmers, labourers etc. Often called familiarly: 'Wellies'.

The idea is to find out as much as you can about the famous people on the banknotes by asking each other questions. Take it in turns to be asked questions.

When you have finished, discuss what you did with the rest of the class.

---

93 You are staying at a hotel. You have just come out of the bathroom and found that all your money, documents, clothes and belongings have been stolen. All the hotel staff seem to be off duty. It is six o'clock in the morning and your plane to London leaves at nine – you must be on that plane.

Try to get the guest(s) in the next room to agree to help you. Before you begin, make some notes of the problems you have to solve. For example you have lost your passport and airline ticket, ... you are a funny size and the other guests' clothes won't fit you, ... this means that you can't leave your room.

Begin by calling for help.

When you have finished, discuss what you did with the rest of the class, then look at activity 100.

94 You and your friend are going on holiday together. You have been looking through the brochures and this hotel has caught your eye:

Sousse, capital of the Sahel (the shore) region, is one of the most important cities in Tunisia as well as being one of the country's leading resorts. To the north of the old walled city (medina) and its busy harbour are the resort's many modern hotels bordering a seemingly endless ribbon of fine, pale sand. You can go water-skiing, and sailing boats can be hired. There's also horse-riding on the sands, and if you feel adventurous you can try a camel ride. All our hotels have, or share, tennis courts. In the evenings you can join the locals and other visitors at a café on the central Farhat Hached Square and simply relax with a mint tea and watch the colourful life of the town pass by. For dancing after dinner there's the Loukala nightclub in the medina. All our hotels have their own discotheque or nightclub where you can dance and sometimes watch an exotic floorshow.

TUNISIA Sousse

HOTEL SALEM TTT

The Moorish-style Hotel Salem stands in sub-tropical gardens leading down to the beach. The centre of Sousse, about three miles away, is easily reached by taxi. This hotel, with its pleasant but quiet atmosphere, is a good choice for a relaxing holiday.

* large swimming pool
* three sun terraces
* bar service
* spacious bar-lounge
* snacks available
* Moorish coffee bar
* choice of menu
* à la carte menu available
* tennis, table-tennis (equipment can be hired)
* football machines, chess, draughts, TV
* discotheque
* shop
* sauna
* cots available for children
* pedalos and horse-riding available on beach

Prices shown are per person in a room with two or three beds, with private shower, w.c., balcony and sea-view. For single room add £2.00 per night.

Full board only
Official Rating: ★★
Hotel Bedrooms: 202

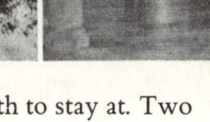

In Sousse ▲

Persuade your friend to accept your choice of hotel for you both to stay at. Two weeks will cost you £150 each with full board.

119

95 This time you are playing the role of your partner's boss. He or she is your assistant.

1 Your assistant seems nervous...
2 Your assistant did something stupid yesterday and you lost your temper. Apologize because he or she is a very good assistant and you were in a bad mood yesterday.

When you have finished look at activity 81.

---

96 You are an accident-prone student staying with an English family. Your hostess has been out for the evening. When she gets back, you have some bad news for her:

The TV seems to have gone wrong. You just turned it on, there was a bang and some smoke, so you quickly turned it off.
The cat seems to be very upset – it has been miaowing all the evening.
You don't know how it happened, but the lock on the front door doesn't seem to work any more.

After your conversation, look at activity 146.

---

97 (You are in group A.) The people in the other group have been getting on your nerves all through this course. The time has come to stop being polite and tactful and to really tell them what you think of them. Decide with the other members of your group what exactly annoys you most about the people in group B. For example:

They ask boring irrelevant questions.
They are very intolerant.
They haven't got a sense of humour – they can't take a joke.
They're always asking for extra homework.
They wear their best clothes every day.
They are excessively punctual.

Add to this list and invent examples of each criticism.

When you are ready, start criticizing them to their faces!

---

98 Here is another subject you feel strongly about:
WORKERS NEED LONGER HOLIDAYS

Again you have three minutes to prepare your arguments. You believe that if workers had longer holidays and shorter hours, more people could be employed and boring routine jobs would be less unpleasant.
Try to make your partners listen to your arguments.

When you have finished, discuss what you did with the rest of the class.

99

You are an expert on Sir Isaac Newton, the man on the £1 note. Study the outline of his life for a few minutes.

ISAAC NEWTON
1642 – 1727

Born Woolsthorpe, Lincolnshire.
Became fellow of Trinity College, Cambridge, in 1667.

He investigated *white light* and found it to be composed of different colours: red, orange, yellow, green, blue, indigo and violet.

He discovered the *binomial theorem* and invented *differential* and *integral calculus.* (It was independently invented by Gottfried Leibnitz in Germany at the same time.)

He began to investigate *gravitation* after seeing an apple fall from a tree. He noticed that it fell towards the earth, not away from it, and concluded that it was being attracted by a force. 1685 published Universal Law of Gravitation. (The popular story is that the apple fell on his head.)

Became President of the Royal Society in 1703. Knighted 1705.
Died 1727, age 85 – buried in Westminster Abbey, London.

During his adult life he wrote an average of 2000 words a day. A newton *is a unit of measurement of force.*

The idea is to find out as much as you can about the famous people on the banknotes by asking each other questions. Take it in turns to be asked questions.

When you have finished, discuss what you did with the rest of the class.

100

You are the personal assistant of B, a business man or woman, who has called you into the office to give you your instructions for the day.
There may be some things that you can't or don't want to do. If you refuse rudely, you may get the sack, so be very *polite* if you are refusing. Make sure you know *exactly* what he or she wants you to do before you agree.

When you have finished, discuss the activity with the rest of the class. Then student C looks at activity 132, while student A looks at activity 2. (If there is no student C, then student A should look at activity 132.)

101

(You are in group C.) Make sure each member of the group has time to say what he or she thinks. Your committee has been asked to prepare a report on:

YOUR MAIN DIFFICULTIES WITH ENGLISH PRONUNCIATION

Your discussion should include: sounds you find difficult, stress and intonation, expressing attitude by your tone of voice, your feelings about a foreign accent, different individual students having different problems etc.

When you are ready, listen to group A's report and group B's report and comment on them. Then make your report and ask the rest of the class for their comments on it.

102

Before you start, spend a little time preparing your ideas on the topic of MARRIAGE. Here are some ideas to start you thinking:

FOR
1 Stable upbringing for children
2 Taxes are lower for married couples
3 Parents like their children to get married...

AGAINST
1 Unreasonable to promise how you will want to spend the rest of your life
2 Couples are tied together by law for life
3 Divorce causes unhappiness for all concerned...

When you are ready, listen to what your partner has to say on his or her topic – ask your partner to explain his or her opinions as exactly as possible.

When you have discussed your partner's topic thoroughly, introduce your own topic.

When you have finished, discuss what you did with the rest of the class.

103

Your friend seems very depressed. Ask what's wrong and listen sympathetically. Try to cheer your friend up. Perhaps offer some advice or suggest something to take your friend's mind off his or her problems.

When your friend seems happier, look at activity 152.

104 You are an expert on making yogurt. Study these instructions first:

How to make your own YOGURT....

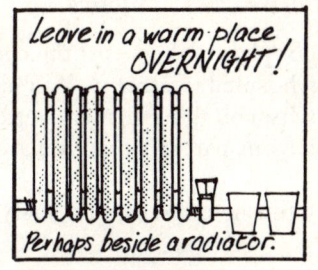

- Heat milk and boil for one minute...
- Allow to cool to about 40°C. (blood heat).
- Add a little YOGURT as a starter + stir!
- Pour into little pots...
- Leave in a warm place OVERNIGHT! Perhaps beside a radiator.
- or best of all, use a VACUUM FLASK and...
- Next morning: yogurt!
- put it in the fridge to COOL
- serve with BROWN sugar or-try it with HONEY ...LOVELY!!

First, listen to your partner who will explain how to do something. Ask questions and get a detailed explanation. Imagine you have no idea about the subject. Repeat the instructions back to your partner to show you have fully understood.

Then explain to your partner how to make yogurt. Do not look at the instructions above while you are explaining.

---

105 It's your flat and while your friends are here you want to get as much done as possible. Begin by making a list of the things *you* think need doing – don't forget food: you all need to eat at midday and in the evening and there's no time to go out for a meal.

When you are ready, welcome your friends to your flat and decide together what needs doing and who is going to do what. Make sure everyone does an equal share of the work and remember that it's usually more efficient for one person to do a job alone than to have two or three doing the same job (too many cooks spoil the broth).

106 (You are student C.) Begin by helping A and B to solve their problems. Then play this role yourself:

You are a millionaire and you get hundreds of begging letters every day asking for money. You do want to give some of your money to people who need it, but how can you decide who needs it most? You just want a clear conscience and a quiet life.

When your problem has been discussed, advise D how to solve his or her problem.

When you have all finished, discuss what you did with the rest of the class.

---

107 This is a subject you feel *very* strongly about:
CIGARETTES SHOULD BE TAXED HIGHER

Because, for example, smokers cost the community so much in working days lost due to illness and in hospital treatment. You have three minutes to think and make notes of the reasons why you think that cigarettes should be more expensive.
Try to convince your partners that you are right – make them listen to your reasons.

When you have finished, discuss and analyse your performance. Then look at activity 39.

---

108 Now it's your turn to go round looking for someone to agree to your requests. Remember that you must be polite. All the people you ask are strangers. You must get help with the first problem before you move on to the second.

1 You need 5p for a phone call, but you only have a 50p piece.
2 You need to know today's date.
3 Your nose in running and you haven't got a handkerchief or any tissues.
4 You don't understand the word 'acquaintance'.
5 You've just bought some sweets but you can't open the packet.
6 You're lost in a part of town you don't know.
7 You can't read a sign on the other side of the road.
8 You're in a shop trying to find a birthday card for a friend. You can't decide which card to buy.
9 It's time for everyone to stop work. When your partner has agreed to stop, you can sit down.

109

Your partner has some information about the early career of the Beatles. Find out the facts missing from the information sheet below by asking appropriate questions. Treat your partner as an acquaintance, not as a close friend.

```
THE BEATLES 1956 - 1964

Richard ....... (Ringo Starr) born 7.7.40
John ....... Lennon           born ......, died .......80
Paul McCartney                born ......
George Harrison               born ......

1956-58 Their early groups were called: the ........., Wump and the Werbles,
        the Rainbows, John and ............ .
1959    John, Paul, George and two others became the Beatles.
1960    They played at the ...... Club in Liverpool and in ....... .
1961    Brian Epstein (manager of .............) became their manager.  He made
        them .......... and ............... .
1962    Beatles signed up by ............ of Parlophone Records.  He became the
        producer of all their recordings.  ........... joined the group,
        replacing the two others who had left.  .......... released - went to
        number .. in the charts.
1963    Five number 1 records: Please Please Me, ................, ................,
        .............., I Want to Hold Your Hand.  First tours of Britain.  Start
        of '...........'.  Crowds ........ .

        Sunday Times: '... greatest ........................'
        ...............: '... our best exports.'
1964    Success in ... .  Tours of .............., ......, ......... .  First film
        ................. directed by Richard Lester.
```

When you are satisfied with your partner's answers, thank him or her politely and then look at activity 124.

110

This time you stay where you are while different people ask you to do things. If they ask politely enough to persuade you, agree to their requests – but you can ask *why* they want you to do something.

After the first request, stand up and wait for your next visitor. Treat everyone as a friend, but they are not very close friends.

Another student will tell you what to do when you have finished.

111 Look at this report of a simple conversation. Work *alone* and write down in dialogue form the actual words that were spoken. Begin like this:

Henry: I'm going to visit my mother tomorrow.
Paula: But I've planned to spend the day shopping.

Henry said that he was going to visit his mother the next day, but Paula replied that she had planned to spend the day shopping. Henry suggested that they should travel to town together and spend the morning as each had intended. He asked where he could meet Paula at the end of the morning and when she didn't answer he wondered if she had heard his question. She assured him that she had heard him but she was thinking. When there was still no answer Henry said he would have to go but he would meet Paula by the bus station, and Paula agreed that that was a good idea.

When you have finished, give your written dialogue to your partner. Ask your partner to write a report giving only the main points of the conversation (without looking at this page, of course). Your partner will ask you to do the same with his or her dialogue.

When you have both finished, compare your report with the report your partner started with in activity 46. Discuss the differences.

---

112 Last Saturday afternoon you decided to give a party for your friends the same evening. It was a great success.
Greet the one friend you didn't invite.

When your conversation is finished, discuss this activity with the rest of the class.

---

113 You've just been accused of shoplifting in a department store. The store detective was rude and didn't apologize for making a mistake. You complained to the manager but he told you you should have kept your receipt.
Tell your friend how angry you are.

Look at activity 88, next.

114

Your partner is going to play three different roles – friend, boss and landlady – while you ask for permission to do the things listed in an appropriate way. Give reasons if necessary and try not to take *no* for an answer!

1 Ask your friend to let you open a window. It's terribly stuffy.
2 Ask your boss to let you make a short local phone call to the garage to see if your car is ready. You want to use the office phone.
3 Ask your landlady to let one of your friends come and watch a programme on BBC2 this evening.
4 Ask your friend to let you open another window. It's still rather stuffy.
5 Ask your boss if you can use the office phone again – this time to ring your brother in another town.
6 Ask your landlady if *two* of your friends can come and watch her TV.
7 Ask your friend to let you open all the windows in the room. You are feeling dizzy.
8 Ask your boss if you can use the office phone again. This time you have to make a very urgent personal call to your sister overseas.
9 Ask your landlady if a third friend can now come to watch the programme on BBC2.

When you have finished, discuss what you did with your teacher and the rest of the class.

115

One of your flat-mates, John, is always listening to records of opera on your hi-fi. Last night it woke you up at 2 a.m. You hate opera. Also, he never does his share of the washing-up and cleaning.
Tell your friend how angry you are with John.

Look at activity 18, next.

116

You always park your car in the street because you haven't got a garage. Your neighbour is a bad driver and always has difficulty driving in and out of his or her garage.
Your neighbour is about to knock at your door.

Try to satisfy your neighbour's complaints, then look at activity 138.

117 You have cut this advertisement out of a newspaper. The product advertised seems really good – great value for money in fact. Persuade your partners to spend their money on this:

SPORTS, OVERNIGHT, BEACH, SCHOOL, BUSINESS.
THE EVERYTHING BAG, ONLY £8.95. (+p&p)

Here, at the special offer price of only £8.95, is the one bag that does the work of many. Not only can you use it for literally every purpose but, with its *six* separate zippered compartments, it can hold a staggering amount of luggage... papers... sports kit.

The secret of the Everything Bag's capacity to stay looking smart, whatever you use it for, is a remarkable man-made material that looks and feels like the softest luxury leather. But unlike leather, it won't scuff. It's difficult to stain. And most marks simply wipe off, leaving your bag like new.

Use it for the beach one day, and a business trip the next. For overnight stays, you can safely carry your own clothes alongside wet baby things. The kids can use it for muddy football kit *and* schoolbooks.

Ideal for cameras, too.
Weighs only 24oz, holds 45lb.

You can fold the bag down to a slim 1" thick, and pack it away inside other luggage without harming it... it weighs only 24 ounces, measures 15" x 8¾" x 11¾" fully open. Yet it safely holds 45lb, and you'll be amazed at the way it swallows even bulky items like a jacket and trousers or a tennis racket.

6 separate zippered compartments.

There are six compartments to keep everything you need easily to hand, and all have strong metal zippers with nylon ribbing underneath to take the strain.

The main compartment takes your big luggage. On one side, there's a compartment with a waterproof lining for wet swimming things or baby things to be carried alongside dry clothes. On the other side, there's a compartment that's perfect for business documents or a thin attache case. And three smaller pockets are ideal for underwear, toilet articles, or travel documents that you want to keep instantly at hand. All the compartment interiors are easy to wipe clean.

Shoulder or hand carrying.

The strap, with built in name and address tag and strong nickel-plated rings, can be adjusted for either shoulder or hand carrying.

Fully guaranteed. Money back offer.

The Everything Bag carries the maker's full one year guarantee. And, if you're not totally delighted with it, simply return it within 30 days for a full refund. So post off the coupon today.

Big and tough enough for sports use... still stays smart.

To: Scotcade Ltd., 33-34 High Street, Bridgnorth, Shropshire WV16 4HG.
Please send me _____ Everything Bag(s) (TB--)
at £9.90 each (inc. 95p p&p).
I enclose my Cheque/Postal Order for
£_____
or debit my Barclaycard No._____
Signature_____
NAME_____ (Block Letters)
ADDRESS_____
CT/01/10
Scotcade Ltd., Registered Office, 14 Grosvenor Place, London SW1. Registered No. 1148225 England. Allow 21-28 days for delivery. Delivery U.K. exc. Channel Islands.

Scotcade Ltd.
33-34 High Street, Bridgnorth, Shropshire WV16 4HG.

© Scotcade Ltd 1978.

Take it in turns with the others in your group to talk about the product you have seen advertised.

---

118 Your friend seems to be in a bad temper. Find out what's the matter and try to calm him or her down.

Look at activity 113, next.

119

Your two friends have agreed to spend the weekend with you. Here are your ideas on what to do:

SATURDAY Get up early. Catch bus to country.
Walk back to town (stop at pub for lunch on the way).
Evening: cinema (tell them about really good film that's on).

SUNDAY Morning: go and visit your teacher (tell them about the coffee and cakes you had last time you went to his or her house).
Spend afternoon in the kitchen preparing super meal for the evening (tell them the dishes you have in mind).
Evening: invite 3 more friends for dinner you've prepared.

Take it in turns to present your plans to each other. Be enthusiastic!
Decide which plan sounds best. If necessary, work out a compromise plan.

120

This time you are playing the role of your partner's boss. He or she is your assistant.

1 Your assistant has just come back very late from the bank (he or she took £20 in change in for you). Find out why your assistant spent so long on such a short journey.
2 You asked your assistant to work late this evening to finish an urgent report. Now the report isn't needed. (You know he or she had to cancel a date to stay and work.)

When you have finished, report what happened to the rest of the class.

121

You have just failed your driving test. You had just bought a new car and booked the car ferry for a motoring holiday. Your companions can't drive. You'll have to cancel your holiday and you can't get the money back at such short notice. Tell your friend.

When you feel better, look at activity 37.

122

Listen to your friend's ideas and pretend to be indifferent. All your partner's plans seem really boring to you. Even talking to other people in the class bores you stiff!

123

In this part of the activity it's your turn to play a role. Get together with the other student As, choose a role from this list and make a badge or label for yourself:

I am your	BOSS		I am an	ELDERLY STRANGER
I am your	ASSISTANT		I am a	CHILD you know
I am a	STRANGER your own age		I am the	HOTEL RECEPTIONIST
I am your	LANDLADY		I am your	HEADMASTER

Agree to what people ask if they are polite enough and the request seems reasonable. You can ask *why*.

Another student will tell you what to do when you have finished.

124

This time you are an expert on the later career of the Beatles. Your partner will try to find out what you know. Treat your partner as an acquaintance, not as a close friend.

THE BEATLES 1965 - 1970

1965 Tour of USA - $304,000 from Shea Stadium concert in New York. We Can Work it Out was their 10th British number 1. Second film Help! in colour directed by Richard Lester.

1966 World tour, including Japan. John Lennon: '... the Beatles are now more popular than Christ.' Last live concert, San Francisco. Revolver released.

1967 Sergeant Pepper's Lonely Hearts Club Band praised by critics and fans. All You Need is Love seen on TV by 150 million viewers. Brian Epstein committed suicide. TV film Magical Mystery Tour described by critics as 'amateurish rubbish'.

1968 Studying in India with the Maharishi. The Beatles 'White Album' disappointed many fans. Excellent cartoon film Yellow Submarine based on Beatles songs, directed by George Dunning.

1969 Disagreement between John and Paul. John married Yoko Ono, Paul married Linda Eastman. Abbey Road recorded.

1970 Premiere of film Let it Be - no Beatles attended. Paul: '... I didn't leave the Beatles, the Beatles have left the Beatles - but no one wants to be the one to say the party's over.' The four Beatles began their solo careers.

When your partner is satisfied with the answers you have given, discuss what you did with the rest of the class.

125

You have been asked to give a talk to all the students in the school about your country. The magazines and brochures you wanted haven't arrived. The talk begins in ten minutes. You haven't prepared it well enough. You can't get out of it now — everyone is depending on you. Tell your friend.

When you feel better, discuss what you did with the rest of the class. That's the end of this activity.

126

(You are student B.) Begin by listening to A's problem. Help her to solve it by giving advice. Then play this role yourself:

You are a 30-year-old bachelor and your father has just died. Your mother doesn't want to live on her own and she wants to come and live with you. You have two married sisters but they both live in Australia and don't want her there. There are no other relations. You're afraid that if you refuse to take her she will become very upset and ill. The trouble is that you really don't get on very well with her. What should you do?

When your partners have solved your problem, advise C and D how to solve their problems.

When you have all finished, discuss what you did with the rest of the class.

127 Your friend seems angry again. He or she seems to have an injured leg. Find out what happened and be sympathetic.

Look at activity 71 when your friend is calmer.

128 Your neighbour has two young children who are very noisy. They scream and shout even at midnight. Your neighbour doesn't seem to care about their screaming.
You have just had a sleepless night as a result. Go and complain – but *don't* be aggressive! Knock at the door first.

When you're satisfied, look at activity 129.

129 You have a beautiful dog which you love very much. It sometimes barks at strangers but it would never hurt anyone. Your neighbour is about to knock at your door.

Try to satisfy your neighbour's complaint and then look at activity 34.

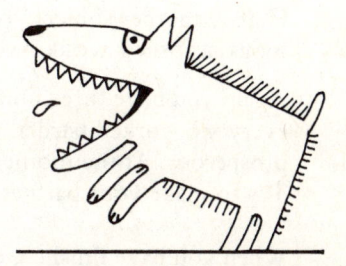

130 You waited for John at the bus stop for thirty minutes but he never arrived. By that time you were late and had to take a taxi. John is always unpunctual.
Tell your friend how angry you are with John.

Look at activity 118, next.

131 (You are in group B.) The people in the other group have been getting on your nerves all through this course. The time has come to stop being polite and tactful and to really tell them what you think of them. Decide with the other members of your group what exactly annoys you most about the people in group A. For example:

They always ask stupid questions.
They laugh at silly jokes all the time.
They're always late for lessons.
They never do their homework.
They wear scruffy, dirty clothes.
They don't seem to think anything is important.

Add to this list and invent examples of each criticism.

When you are ready, start criticizing them to their faces!

132

You are planning a large picnic in the country for your class. Your friends are no good at organizing, so you have taken charge and now you have to tell the others what to do. Here are some of the things that need arranging:

TRANSPORT: enough cars for the whole class and perhaps their guests
FOOD: buy food, prepare and cook suitable dishes, get cutlery and plates
DRINK: plenty of different drinks to suit all tastes – hot, cold, alcoholic and soft
ENTERTAINMENT: music (at least a guitar and cassette player), sports equipment (at least football and badminton stuff)
INVITATIONS: contact all guests by phone or personally. Don't forget your teachers!
WET WEATHER: alternative plan?
MONEY: get money from everybody *before* the picnic

When you have finished, discuss the differences between the *three* parts of this activity.

133

Here is another subject you feel strongly about:
WORKERS DON'T WORK HARD ENOUGH

Again you have three minutes to prepare your arguments. You believe that if everyone worked harder, productivity would rise and the country would be more prosperous. At the moment all workers are much too lazy.
Try to make your partners listen to your arguments.

When you have finished, discuss what you have done with the rest of the class.

134

This time you are playing the role of your partner's assistant. He or she is your boss.

1 You have just made a transatlantic telephone call without your boss's permission. If you don't tell your boss first, someone else will. Break it gently because your boss told you never to use the office phone for private calls.
2 You did something rather stupid yesterday and your boss got angry ...

When you have finished, look at activity 120.

135 Begin by studying this strip cartoon. Decide how you can make your narration as interesting as possible. Add *detail* and *dialogue*. Imagine what had happened *before* the first scene and what happened *after* the last scene.

When you are ready, tell your partner the story. Then listen to his or her story and ask plenty of questions to get as much detail as possible.

136 (You are still in group A.) This time it's your turn to be the passive partner. Stand up and wait for people from group B to start conversations with you. Let them ask the questions and finish each conversation.

After a number of conversations, your teacher will tell you to stop. Then there will be time for you to discuss what you did with the rest of the class.

---

137 You always drink orange juice and only smoke a few cigarettes a day. You don't see why you should offer everyone else at the bar expensive drinks and give away lots of cigarettes to heavy smokers.
Greet your friend and see what he or she has to say.

When your conversation is finished, look at activity 89.

---

138 Your neighbour's TV is always on – all day and all night. This keeps you awake because the volume is always too high. Your neighbour is *very* deaf, so you will need to shout.
Knock at the door first.

When you are satisfied, look at activity 137.

---

139 Find out what's the matter with your friend.

When you have cheered your friend up, look at activity 125.

---

140 Your partner will begin by telling you a story. Keep interrupting with questions. Later you will have to tell him or her this story, so read it through now and try to memorize the main points. You should *not* just read it aloud, but tell it from memory!

One afternoon a big wolf waited in a dark forest for a little girl to come along carrying a basket of food to her grandmother. Eventually a little girl with a basket of food did come along and the wolf found out from her where she was going and disappeared into the forest. After a long walk the little girl arrived at her grandmother's house, opened the door and saw someone in her grandmother's bed wearing her grandmother's clothes. She soon realized that it was the wolf! . . .
Luckily, little girls nowadays are better prepared than they used to be, so she took out her revolver and shot the wolf dead.   *(Adapted from a story by James Thurber)*

When you have finished, discuss what you did with the rest of the class.

141 You and your friend are going on holiday together. You have been looking through the brochures and this hotel caught your eye:

Austria
St.Wolfgang

St. Wolfgang, one of the most popular summer resorts in Austria, is known to music lovers the world over – thanks to the White Horse Inn! You'll find lots to do in this picturesque resort where life centres around the beautiful Wolfgangsee. You can swim, fish, sail, water-ski, hire a rowing or motor-boat or go for a cruise on a lake steamer. Tennis and crazy-golf are also available and there are many beautiful walks in the area. The town itself, with its frescoed houses and shops and narrow cobbled streets, is a delightful place to explore – you can watch a wood-carver at work, or visit the Pilgrimage Church which has a magnificent 16th century altar. During your stay you should also make the unforgettable trip up the Schafberg mountain (5,850 feet) by rack and pinion railway, and enjoy the magnificent views from its summit.

White Horse Inn

The White Horse Inn T T T T T

The White Horse Inn is in an excellent position, in the town centre right beside the lake. This friendly hotel, which consists of two buildings, has a heated indoor swimming-pool, fitness-room, sauna, massage and solarium as well as comfortable lounges, bar and attractive dining-rooms overlooking the lake.
The hotel also has a small outdoor children's pool, electric boat and sailing dinghy.
Prices shown are per person **for half board** in a room with two or three beds, with washbasin.
Supplements (per person per night):
Single room £3.00; private bath, w.c., balcony and lake-view £3.00; full board £2.50.
Official Rating: A
Hotel Bedrooms: 65

Persuade your friend to accept your choice of hotel for you both to stay at. Two weeks will cost you £160 each with full board.

135

142 Before you start, spend a little time preparing your ideas on the topic of EXAMS. Here are some ideas to start you thinking:

FOR
1 Needed for paper qualifications
2 Objective assessment of ability
3 Motivates pupils to work hard...

AGAINST
1 Fear of failing exams is unhealthy
2 Unfair to pupils who get nervous
3 Written exams don't assess real-life skills...

When you are ready, introduce your topic to your partner and say what you think.

When your topic has been discussed thoroughly, listen to what your partner has to say about his or her topic.

When you have both finished, discuss what you did with the rest of the class.

---

143 Your group is planning a bicycle tour of Europe. You are going for one month and you want to spend as little money as possible and see as much as possible.
Decide what equipment, clothes etc. you are going to take and tell the rest of the class. If you disagree about an item, report it as a possible or probable item for inclusion. Give reasons why you need or don't need each item.
You are definitely going on this tour, by the way – so don't spend time deciding if it's a good idea to go or not!

✓ = Yes, definitely
✓? = Yes, probably
?? = Perhaps
✗? = No, probably not
✗ = No, definitely not

---

144 Begin by playing this role and ask your partners to give you advice:

You are a 16-year-old girl and your father is very strict. He says you must be home at 8 o'clock in the evening and you are not allowed to go out with boys. He says you can do what you like when you're 18, but not at your age. You feel like leaving home but your mother would be heartbroken if you did. What should you do?

When your partners have discussed your problem, advise them how to solve their problems.

When you have all finished, discuss what you did with the rest of the class.

---

145 Your friend seems to be in a bad mood. Find out what's wrong and be sympathetic.

Look at activity 127 when your friend is calmer.

146 Now it's your turn to play the role of the housewife. You have just returned home after a really pleasant evening at the Social Club (where you won £50). Find out from your student:

What the funny smell in the house is.
If he or she enjoyed the meal you left in the oven.
What message Mrs Brown left when she phoned.
What time he or she fetched your little son, Billy, from Mrs Green's.

When you have both finished, discuss what you did with the rest of the class.

---

147 Try to interest your friend in these ideas:

Reading a good book you've just read.
Watching TV this evening.
Going for a fast drive in a new car.
Going for a walk this evening.
Having a discussion about the political situation.

When you have succeeded in arousing his or her interest, discuss what you did with the rest of the class.

---

148 You have several pieces of bad news for your friends. Break each piece of news gently and say how disappointed you are. When your friends tell you their bad news, try to be sympathetic.

1 Your teacher has invited you to dinner, but not your friends.
2 Your car won't start, so you can't give your friends a lift home.
3 You promised to record a TV programme about your country, but it was cancelled.
4 You got the last seat on the plane. Your friends couldn't get seats, so they can't go.
5 You tried phoning your friends to invite them to London with you but you couldn't get through. So you went there alone and had a miserable time.

---

149 Read this simple story and try to memorize the main points. When you are ready, tell your partner the story and be prepared for interruptions. Tell the story from memory – *don't* read it aloud!

Once there was an old king. He asked all his wise men to summarize all the knowledge in the world into one library of books. When they had done that, he told them to go back and summarize it into one book. Years later they returned with the single book and he told them to summarize it into one chapter. Then one page. Then one paragraph. Then one sentence. By the time this was done there was only one very old wise man still alive. The king told him to summarize the sentence into one word. He spent years on the task and, as he was dying, he wrote down the one word and gave it to his servant and died. The servant brought the piece of paper to the king ... but no-one could read the old man's writing!

When you have told your story, listen to your partner's story and keep interrupting with questions.

150 Now it's your turn to play the role of stranger. Remain seated when people come to you with their problems. Then agree or refuse to do what you are asked. Remember that if you refuse you must do so *politely* and give a good reason.

Here is some information about your role, which may influence whether you agree or refuse.

1 You have plenty of small change.
2 You're not sure what today's date is.
3 You have just bought a packet of tissues.
4 You dislike explaining English words to foreigners.
5 You have a sweet tooth.
6 You're good at giving directions.
7 You have left your glasses at home.
8 You have very good taste.
9 You would like to go on doing this activity.

---

151 (You are in group A.) In this activity you have to pretend to be very confident. The idea is for you to start a series of conversations with different people in group B. In real life you have to be quite brave to do this – practice in class will help you to become confident. Treat the classroom as a place where you can *experiment*!

End each conversation by saying: 'Well, it's been nice talking to you, but I really must be going now. Sorry to rush off.' Then find another member of group B to start a conversation with. Stand up and find someone to talk to now! When your teacher gives you a signal, stop talking and look at communication activity 136.

---

152 Now it's your turn to be unhappy. It's been one of those days – tell your friend about these events which have made you feel really depressed:

Your car wouldn't start this morning.
You were late for work.
Your boss was angry.
You have to work late tonight.
You can't go to the theatre now.
You've just dropped coffee on your lap.
You've come out without any money.
You've got a headache.

When you feel happier, discuss what you did with the rest of the class.

---

153 Listen to your friend's ideas and pretend to be indifferent. All your friend's plans seem really boring to you. Even this type of activity bores you to death!